Wrong Kind of Love
A story on narcissistic abuse

Taylor Routley

Mending Hearts Books—Dubuque, IA
ISBN: 978-0-578-82218-1
Library of Congress Control Number: 2020925027
Title: *Wrong Kind of Love*
Author: Taylor Routley
Digital distribution | 2020
Paperback | 2020

This is a work of fiction. The characters, names, incidents, places, and dialogue are products of the author's imagination, and are not to be construed as real.

About the Author

Taylor Routley has a degree in accounting and loves researching topics she is passionate about. Writing, art and music have always been her real passions, but reading studies and books on psychology and emotional abuse has become a hobby of hers. She graduated her accounting degree with honors as a member of the National Society of Leadership and Success back in 2017. The author is a mother of a beautiful little girl and a fiancé scheduled to be married in May. She loves running and spending time with her daughter when she's not working or writing.

Understanding

Seeking closure is more poisonous than we tend to understand. We can crave a final statement that will tie the confusion and pain together. This is such a rarity that even when it seems to happen, it doesn't actually tie our wounds together. It just answers one of the several questions that lie dormant in the back of our minds': one of the building blocks of our own misery. Getting these loose answers and hearing these statements of broken promises, supposed regret, and sometimes even unexpected ambivalence from your manipulator can tend to do so much more harm than leaving well enough alone. However, the closure that you need; the closure that does not come from their mouth, comes when you least expect it. I have spent a long time debating if I should tell my story, because of not only other people's opinions from my own life, but also the chance that the person this story is about would actually pick up a book and read this. Yet, regardless of the painful memories, it crossed my mind that I could help someone that was in my shoes.

I know what it's like to lay in a dark room alone dwelling on the days sorrow as I ask myself why this is happening to me, and what I need to do to get out of the situation I had found myself in. I know what it is like to feel trapped even though I knew deep down that I could walk out that door. I know what it is like to feel like your legs do not work, as irrationality is taking control over every piece of your mind. I spent years being manipulated by a man that had everyone around him fooled, and I know how easy it is to have your brain warped. More importantly, I want to share how I managed to find a new and better me than I have ever known.

As miserable as I was, sometimes the pain and situations I found myself in were almost wretchedly poetic. He made me want to run away but hold his hand while I ran. I felt a need to jump a sinking ship, but then try to steer it to safety. I let go of everything I thought I believed in more and more as time went on. The ups and downs were always severe; there was never an in between. I always loved music and used it as my first measure of trying to feel when I was numb. That feeling we have when we listen to a song and feel the lyrics move a piece of us that we have never met before. You know the feeling; it's beautiful and you want to make everyone else listen to it. It hurts realizing you cannot replay that "song" with a relationship. He made me want to live, and then he made me want to die. It feels like such an empty space we float around in when we do not have answers or solutions to make our hearts just feel better. I will be honest, there were so many bad times that in some twisted way, I almost felt like I had to be sad or angry to feel normal.

The words *broke up* hurt. You hear two seemingly simple words and fill with rage and sadness because no one outside of your mind understands that there are millions of little stories, hopelessness, and tears in those two words. I've gone through breakups before, and I cried over it for a few days, then I picked myself up and moved on. It was not like that with John. I wanted to say, "I'm bleeding inside and don't know how to ask for help, because I don't understand how it's possible to feel dead while I am still breathing." Or maybe, "Do you have any idea how hard it was to leave?" And that alone was agonizing. You give effort and you explain to close friends, maybe even your therapist, what happened and why you feel numb, but you feel like a broken record that is playing for an empty stadium. I felt pathetic because I had never understood mental torment or such painful confusion and self-hatred until this relationship, and I could never find the words to make it sound like what was happening was not in my head. Most of this happened behind closed doors, so how are you supposed to explain to people that the fairytale they see is really a horror story at home?

I am a healthy and happy mother to a beautiful little girl that I never thought I would have. I bought a house recently, which I never thought I would be able to do. Even better, I am a fiancé to a man that is so loving, and so kind to me, that I believe love is real again. I see it every single day in his words, his actions, and the way he fathers our daughter. I remember a time just a couple short years ago when everywhere I turned, I saw grey. It was so hard to find a reason to keep going, and that wasn't something I could openly share with just anyone. I spent years being told I was unstable, crazy, and needy; yet he wouldn't let me go without psychological warfare, no matter what I did or said. I found my happy, and I found my ever-after. It existed and I almost gave up on it, so many times.

I understand what it's like searching for a voice, anywhere, that knows because they have been there. You want to hear, "That happened to me, too." But you do not seem to find your snowflake situation to relate to and use as a template to move forward. Now that I have found peace, I can see that it is not supposed to be like that. The point of this is that you do not need that template. You are in your own battle, unlike any other, and you unfortunately will not always get a guide on how to fight it. However, there are others like you that have fought and won. I want to share my story and make sure someone finds their way back to themselves; whole. This book is not a how-to manual, it is just a familiar voice that might help someone understand it is possible to really step back.

There are many types of emotional and psychological abuse that I have done a lot of research on. I spent 5 years being tormented by a narcissistic, self-centered, manipulative man, and I had absolutely no idea that it was happening until it was far too late. The teeth of addictive infatuation were already set so deep, that by the time I felt their stabbing, I did not know how to release their grip. It is so unbelievably hard to leave a relationship like this and expect to be the same person or even stable once it's over. The time healing after leaving him was not easy and I just recently found a successful way to start really healing from it. Don't ever let anyone tell you that your feelings were wrong, that you were the problem, or that you imagined what happened to you. No one except you and your tormenter really know what happened, and no one can take that from you.

Chapter One
Infatuated

December 10th, 2013 – around 7AM, is when John messaged me for the first time. God bless Facebook. Not many people believe that I remember the time and date he messaged me, but because I worked in a group home taking care of elderly disabled adults - I kept very tight logs so I guess I was good at remembering events. I was roughly two months from my 20h birthday and was not looking for any type of relationships with anyone. The number of hours I was working at the time consumed my social life, so it just did not appeal to me to be involved with someone; I liked my alone time. Up until a few months ago, today in 2020, I would have given anything to go back in time and tell myself not to respond. But I did, and that is why this story exists. I know that I made mistakes down the line because no one is perfect. It took two of us to dance, I feel it is important say that.

John was endearing, handsome, and I really did not see a reason to not respond. It took a few days, but I did agree to meet him at his mother's where he lived at the time. It was about 10 at night when I got off work and was heading to his mom's. I got lost and called him with all the nerves in the world. This was the first time I had heard his voice and my stomach seemed to fill with lead. I remember scrambling to find the right words and almost forgot immediately why I even called him. After being navigated about for a few minutes, I found the town home and parked my car out front. I nervously walked up the sidewalk and came around the corner where he was waiting for me at the door. He was very handsome that night – big blue eyes that seemed inviting and dimples that took my eyes immediately. I went inside where we just watched TV and talked about ourselves. I stayed for about an hour and a half and said goodnight and went home.

A few weeks went by and I went over to hang out every few nights. Things were great honestly; I was smitten. John was kind, he even asked me if he could kiss me the first time he did. This relationship really came down to the bad vastly outweighing the good. However, I can see today which red flags I chose to not see, and which ones flew right over my head. The first night John and I slept together was not planned and happened very suddenly with little thought. I didn't feel immediate regret, until some weeks later. This was the night I started bleeding in his moms bathroom from what I thought was an ovarian cyst rupturing. I have had many of them prior to this moment, so I was not shocked. Well, I later found out it was a miscarriage. John took me to the hospital where I found out the news, alone, as I had him go out to the waiting room. He wanted to stay with me, but I was embarrassed and holding back tears from the pain I was in. When I told him what actually happened as he was taking me back to his mom's to retrieve my car, he was very silent.

A few days after the incident, I was at the gym feeling fine even with the cramping, when he texted me. I remember the machine I was on when I opened the message. I cannot remember the exact text, but it was basically that he almost ruined his life with this event and did not want to see me anymore. I told him fine – it is cool, whatever. I did run to my moms and cry pretty hard that night. About a week later, I decided to go to Chicago to spend the weekend with my aunt, uncle, and cousins. Now, prior to this Saturday morning drive to Chicago, he had texted me a few random times with pointless messages that made me feel really confused on what he wanted. I tried to act like I did not become crazy about him in those couple weeks and just didn't respond. My favorite one had to be about 5 days after he dumped me when he sent me a selfie he took after shaving a goatee on himself asking, "new look?" trying to engage me in conversation. This is what they do, they need the attention, and they need it from you. I do not remember what I said, something passive like, "nice," and left it alone.

My aunt and uncle got me and my cousins tickets to the B96 bash in Chicago, so I tried to just focus on that. I still remember almost driving off the road when John texted me out of the blue about an hour into my drive. This text informed me that he made a mistake and thinks he had fallen in love with me and was sorry. I was filled with joy, but I knew that I should be filled with anger. I stared at the road for about ten minutes before I responded to him. I responded calmly saying I wanted to continue to see him and we would talk when I got back to town

Sunday. I had a great time in Chicago with my family to the point that I forgot about him until my drive home.

Upon arriving home to my apartment downtown, I texted him to let him know I was back, and I honestly do not remember if I saw him that night or not. Another couple weeks went by and we did continue to see each other. He still lived at his mom's, so we hung out there because my apartment was tiny, and I did not want him to see it because I was embarrassed about not having much. I made plans to hang out with my girlfriend Saturday night the following week and have some drinks since I could not go out with John to the bars. He went out with his guy friends and I was honestly fine with it at the time, I really was. I had my life, and he had his. Lack of trust had not come into the picture yet, at least not on my end.

I was sitting in my girlfriends living room when he texted me asking what I was doing. I told him where I was and what I was doing, and I could tell from how he was responding that he was loaded. He started saying he wanted me to go home and he was going to come over, so after telling him a few times I did not want to drive home after drinking, he kept telling me I needed to go home. When I got there, he was leaning up against the outside door of my apartment building, very drunk, in the dark of downtown. I must admit we both were laughing a little when I walked up to him. I am not sure why he did not go inside considering the front door was always unlocked. I put his arm around my shoulder and realized getting him up the staircase was going to be a challenge. To my surprise, he quickly made it up on his own, mostly.

4

Once I unlocked the door, I led him to my bed where he flopped backwards playfully on his back with his knees bent leaving his feet still planted on the floor. I remember laughing and trying to just scoot him up so he could be fully lying down and comfortable, and then he forcefully shoved me and passed out. I was a little shocked and annoyed because it was a rough swipe at my arm, and he was laughing just a minute ago. He was wasted and clearly just wanted to fall asleep and must have been confused. I told him about it in the morning and he felt terrible, so at the time I felt it was not a big deal.

As coming weeks went by I continued to go over to his mom's to see him. I would get off work around 2PM at this point as I wanted to spend time with him so much that I was constantly switching hours with my lead work. It was not a big deal to her as she wanted second shift anyway. This was around the time I realized he was a big gamer. I would bring dinner over or I would make him dinner at his mom's. A few more days went by and he started to get comfortable, and that is when I started feeling like he did not care if I was interacting with him and he just wanted me present. I got up and left one time without saying anything and he did not realize it for a few hours. When I would bring that night up occasionally, he started to say it never happened, which was angering because I could not tell if he was just denying it from shame, or if he was so good at lying he made himself believe it really had not happened.

Fast forwarding a few months to summertime of 2014, John made the decision to move in with his cousin. We had been seeing each other for a few months now and he was sick of living at his moms. We were seeing each other almost daily at this point. Now, like I mentioned earlier I had my own apartment downtown. It was small, but it was my space. I had only been on this lease for about 8 months and I planned on staying there until it was up. I did stay the night at his cousins almost every night for the first two weeks after he moved in. His cousin Blake and his girlfriend Lana were so kind, and I still think they are even though we do not speak anymore. They were extremely inviting and immediately accepting of me and I cherished that.

The next rough incident with John was the night of Lana's 23rd birthday. There was an event called Kickoff to Summer down at the town clock and it was one of my favorite events in our medium sized town every year. We all pre-gamed and got ready to go at Blake's. Many of us split into two groups and loaded into cabs to head downtown. John was in a great mood but already drunk. I got along with Lana and her friends right away and was excited to have a good time with them. We were downtown for about a half hour and the girls had gotten me a drink or two since I was still only 20. Out of nowhere, John came up and firmly grabbed my wrist and said we were getting a cab. I was confused but realized he was drunk.

He loaded me into a cab as I asked what his problem was. He mumbled something about wanting to spend time alone and not with a bunch of people. We got back to Blake's and he stumbled inside while I followed him, almost completely sober. We got inside and he wanted to be intimate with me, but I kept trying to get him to talk to me about why he was upset. The only sentence I remember clearly to this day was, "I don't like sharing you." I asked him what that meant and explained that I was having a good time.

"I like your friends, isn't that what you want?" I asked.

"I don't like you hanging out with other people when you're with me."

Then he got a bit too rough and when I told him to stop, he did not right away. I had told John weeks prior that I had been sexually assaulted at age 16, and I guess he did not understand that when I say stop I mean it. However, he was drunk enough that getting him to stop was not as easy as it should have been. I am not downplaying what he did, but I can see where he may have thought I was not being serious. He rolled over angry and passed out. I did not want to drive home with even 1 drink in me under-aged, so I cried and fell asleep next to him. The next day, John did not remember any of what happened. This would be the second time he looked at me like I was making the situation up. We went for breakfast before I dropped him off at home. That morning, I drove around for a few hours thinking about what had happened because it did not feel right. It was not about the fact he was hammered and clearly not thinking straight. This was about how he looked at me, grabbed me, and treated me when he felt my attention was being taken off him.

About a month later, roughly the end of June if memory serves correct; this was when he asked me to give up my apartment and move into his cousins. He had 1 bedroom, and the rest was a shared home space.

7

I did not love the idea, but I ended up begging my landlord and moving out early with no lease penalties. I had done my own renovations on my own dime to the efficiency and the landlord was extremely happy with me leaving everything behind. Once I moved everything except my clothing into my mother's garage, I was officially living at Blake's. I knew this moved way too fast, and I knew I was making a mistake, but that did not stop me because of how much I wanted to be with John. We were moving so much faster than I was comfortable with.

I am fully aware that I started the trend of future events. When I say this, I mean I know that my love, or what I thought was love, for John triggered a need to appear as housewife material. The moment I moved into Blake's, I made sure I was doing John's laundry, keeping our room clean and organized, and cooking meals as often as possible. John was happy with what I did and did not show any objections. Now being as I worked 6AM to 2PM Monday through Friday at an adult rehab group home, I was absolutely exhausted when I got done with my shift. That was my official schedule, however, I was almost regularly guilted into at least 50 hours a week at this job. John worked a manual labor job from roughly 7AM to 3PM at the time, so our schedules worked well together. After a couple weeks John started to get distant and I started to wonder internally if he was regretting having me move in, as I had been since the day I agreed.

John's birthday rolled around, and I had no idea what I was supposed to do. We had only been dating for half a year and I was not sure what type of gift to get him or if me getting him an actual gift would be weird. I noticed that most of his clothing was Jordan or Nike brand, so I decided I would get some flashy Jordan shoes for him online. I did not spend much – maybe $120 on these. His birthday rolled around, and I was so excited to give these to him. I got off work and came right home with the shoebox wrapped and the biggest smile on my face. I handed the box to him and he looked disoriented. I waited a few seconds, and he began to open the box. His face never changed, and my smile started to melt away.

"Do you hate them?" I asked.

"They're alright," he said, as he rolled them around in his hand then put them in his closet.

I was absolutely deflated, and I made an excuse to leave because I really just had to cry at that point. Dramatic, right? When I returned home, I acted as though nothing had happened. About 10 days later, roughly, Lana asked me to go to Madison with her to just get out. Her and Blake were having a rough patch and it sounded like a nice way to get her mind off things. I told John I was going, and he barely looked up from his computer. I quickly grabbed my purse and left with Lana. A couple hours went by and John texted me saying we spend too much time together. I said okay, I understood and agreed even though it made me sad. I tried to focus on just having girl-time with Lana, but in the back of my mind I was asking myself what I did wrong. After about an hour, I received another text saying that I was not giving him enough attention. I could not even bring myself to respond right away.

I was in the process of buying John candy at this neat little shop Lana and I found, and now I wanted to throw the candy in the trash and just tell him to get lost. I was being ignored constantly but expected to be present. I know I sound like I was being unreasonable about his gaming, but I do not think I was. I just needed him to grow up enough to show me we mattered. I did return home after our trip and he asked where I was. I was at my friend's house trying to figure out where I would move if he really ended things. He asked me to come home and said we were fine, so I listened and came home where I acted as if nothing had happened, per usual.

July 4th of 2014 was probably the worst 4th of July of my life. I made the decision the night before to go out with John, Blake, Lana, and a lot of their friends. Everyone was so kind, and it was a fun time for the first few hours. We walked along Roosevelt St. and saw a lot of yard parties and had a lot of drinks and laughs. We got to a popular bar by the river where we had collected about 15 friends at that point. The girl in front of me, a close friend of Lana, tossed her ID back at me after passing through the door because we looked enough alike for it to work. The bar was absolutely packed as it lied on the river in perfect view of the fireworks about to go off. Suddenly I heard the bursts in the sky while I had a drink on the back patio, and I spaced off looking up at the fireworks alone. I saw John get shoved by Blake to my left as to suggest *go watch with her*. John came over and put his arm around me and smiled for a moment, and then he was gone. Almost every time we were out of the house, I was the last priority. I did not need John to hold my hand and parade me around, but he was constantly off with other people. It got to a point where I knew that he just wanted to know where I was so that he could do what he wanted. I feel that way because even when he was off with other people, he would constantly be looking over at me.

After a few moments I saw Lana start to freak out about Blake acting like a jerk and she stormed off. I followed her to the road bridge close by and talked with her for a minute. She showed me a text from Blake saying something along the lines of, "no more drama, it's just the boys now." Which kind of lead us to believe that meant Lana and I needed to leave. Lana felt it did not mean anything, but at this point I was annoyed with recent events. I did not even feel like John enjoyed my company anymore; why am I here? I was starting to see parts of John that made me uneasy. I went with Lana, reluctantly, and we found the guys and got a cab. Even after the rude way they were acting, we still went home with them. John would not say anything to me at first. After pushing him enough he told me he was angry that when he came back to find me, I had run off with Lana. I guess I understood and dropped it after apologizing.

In the cab on the way back to Blake's, John said that when he could not find me, some guy scuffed his shoes and made him angry. Thus, he almost got in a fight because he "lost me". I hated how he used to look at me when he was angry; like he was fed up. Regardless, I left his point alone because I was too tired to fight. We arrived home, and we went to bed saying few words to each other. I still remember the scrapes on my ankles from those stupid gladiator sandals I thought would be cute with my dress because I wanted to look cute for him, so that was a waste. We woke up in the morning, and John was barely speaking to me. This was the 4th of July, so obviously we had plans. I felt anger from him, and it felt heavy. So, I gathered some of my things, kept my eyes to the ground, and left with few words.

I decided I would take a drive to the apple orchard my aunt and cousins were at a few hours away. I knew this orchard had little to no cell service, which is what I needed. About a half hour before I lost cell service, that text message I knew was coming popped up on my phone, "I'm sorry." I met his apology with, "It's fine. I'll see you later." Unfortunately, I lost service and could not find my cousins on the property, so I turned around and drove home. I had gotten the quiet alone time I needed at that point. Once I got home, I went to the bedroom and slept. As expected, this situation blew over and we dropped it.

John lasted a handful of months at Blake's and tension started to build. There were just too many people living in one house and I completely understand why we all needed to give Blake and Lana their space back. John, along with his best friend Michael who lived in the lower level, decided to move out. Michael also had a girlfriend that was intermittently staying at Blake's. So, in total, there were 4 of us that were needing to leave quickly. After a few days, John informed me and Michael's girlfriend Jen that they had signed a lease for a trailer. I did not have much to say about this considering they did not even look at the place prior to signing the lease. What was I going to say? Good job?

Time went on and it was not awful living as two couples in a small space. I stuck to the routine and continued to cook and clean and try to spend time with John. I got him tickets to his first NFL game for Christmas, even though the game was in November. He was so happy that he jumped off of the couch and hollered when he opened them. I was filled with joy that I had managed to get genuine joy out of John for something that I did. I counted down the days until we could go for the next couple weeks. We had a great vacation away that weekend. For some reason, every time we left town we always had the best time and never argued. We returned home that Sunday and got ready to start another week. I went to bed happy that night because of how peaceful our weekend had been.

Christmas time came and went. We spent time with our families and exchanged gifts. John had gotten me a diamond necklace; those ones that flicker from movement. I loved it so much that I rarely took it off from that day on. John and I had been having more issues lately, mostly about him not spending time with me. I could not see at the time that this necklace probably would have been given to me anyway even if it was not Christmas time. I never wore jewelry up until that point, and I did not think too deep into the meaning behind the necklace at that moment because it was the first jewelry a man had ever given me. In coming years, he brought that necklace up a lot; about how he had spent so much money on it. Every time he would talk about how much he spent or paying off my necklace, it did not feel like it came from love but from vanity and possession. I found it so hard to look for little moments, little actions, hidden glances from John that would give me just a moment of feeling real love to hang on to. It felt like half the time I was in my own head teetering between being angry and being sad. Then, just like that, December was over.

Chapter Two
Addicted

John and I were coming up on just over a year when I made my first mistake. All 4 of us had been in this trailer for about 7 months, making this about March or April of 2015. I realized I was miserable, and it was not my imagination like John seemed to think it was. My birthday was in February; my 21st. I was now legal, and my friends were inviting me out occasionally. It was almost instantly that I became 21 that John decided neither one of us needed to go out anymore. I did get angry and confused, but I felt like I had to be wrong in my feelings because no one had ever stayed with me this long. All I did was work, cook, clean, and sleep. John came home from work and the gym and just gamed, and then I would see him for a few minutes before bed. So, naturally, I still let myself have a social life and it caused a fight every single time. If I pivoted my expected time to return home in the slightest, or where I was planning on going, he would lose it and give me the silent treatment or be passive aggressive for the entire following day.

I lost my job at the end of 2014 for the simple reasoning that the management team and I did not get along, and some relatively shady things were going on that I was no longer comfortable with. I did find a new job within a few weeks and it was looking to be one of the best things I could have done job wise. I had been working at that job for a couple months and had grown close with a man on my team named Sam. He was cute and seemed interested in me. We just talked a lot at work and texted a good amount after work. At the time, he seemed like his only priority was hearing my pain and my story. I thought I had found an amazing new friend, but today I see what a vulture he was. I had not slept with him, but I knew what I was doing was not right. The worst part about this is at the time I felt like I could not be alone, but I could not stay with John. I tried to break up with John several times when I felt the moment was right, but every time I tried he would start crying and saying things that broke my heart. There was one time that he kept saying, "I want my mom" while he was sobbing on his bed. He grabbed my phone, while crying, and told me he was going to find whoever I was leaving him for. I was not leaving him for anyone other than myself. I was not even leaving him for Sam. That absolutely shook me and I could not walk out. His mom resented me for a while because I tried to leave but would return home within hours or the next morning because of how John would act. I did not understand my addiction to him, but I could not handle the thought of not staying with him.

I later discovered that this man, Sam, was a complete and total sociopath. Sam had perfected the science of projecting what you need right back at you. I needed an attentive man that would love me and show me he cared and valued me, and he put on that exact face. At the time, I had fallen for the false persona he had created for me, extremely hard. I later found out I was one of a few women he was luring in, which I may have deserved. I should have closed one door before opening another but looking back I still do not recognize what was happening to me. As time went on, it became more intense and I still could not figure out how to close my chapter with John.

I was lying and hiding things to try and leave home. I was still being neglected and I was starting to feel crazy. When I would explain that I needed him to spend time with me, or that I felt like he didn't care if I was around him, John would say it was my fault that I did not tell him he gamed too much. When he would cave and skip a night of gaming, he did not seem interested in doing anything I suggested. So, it would end up with us watching a movie he wanted to see. I cannot count how many times I would be at work or with my family and feel like the fog lifted a little when I was not around him. However, when I would return home, I believed him that I was asking too much. I know what I did was wrong, letting Sam into my life in the way that I did. I will forever regret it. I did cut things off with Sam because all I wanted to do was figure out how to get John to look at me and want to be with me. The guilt ate away at me for months. There were times, however, the guilt would be absent. When I say that, I mean it was like I was unintentionally jumping from loving what I thought John could be, to convincing myself he was poison and Sam could rescue me, as twisted as that may seem. One specific time resides in my mind.

We were downtown bar crawling with John's friends the early summer of 2015 prior to moving out of the trailer. I cannot remember why we were out, but we met up with his buddies downtown to drink for whatever reason. Now at this point bear in mind I am 21 years old, and ever since my 21st birthday, things changed a lot. John used to go out with his friends while I went to my friend's or stayed in. Now that I was 21, he claimed he despised the bars and would do whatever he could to keep me from going out. I was never interested in finding another man or flirting at the bars, period. However, he never cared and said that it was suspicious I wanted to go out regardless and that if you are in a relationship it is selfish and wrong to go out alone, even though he had been doing it since we met. The worst part was that when he could go out without me, he would intentionally go to the biggest singles bar we had in town knowing I hated it. To make things better, I tried constantly to get him to go out with me and have fun as a couple, but that was not something that interested him.

That night, we were all out simply having a few drinks between a few different bars. Time passed and John's buddy got way too drunk, so we agreed to take him to my vehicle to rest and possibly take him home. John said he had to use the restroom, so I waited by the front door holding up his buddy. Before I know it the bartender or owner is tossing John at me saying he was using a wall as a bathroom out back. Now, personally I do not think that is a big deal, but she was losing her mind, so I apologized and tried to take my purse from her because she had grabbed it from my chair by the front door. John snapped and yelled at her, storming past me out the front door holding my purse he grabbed from her. As we were out front, I told him I would take my purse and he should take his buddy from me and lead him to my SUV. John grabbed my arm with an extraordinarily strong grip while looking at me like he could not be angrier. I froze because it scared me how hard he was grabbing me, and at that moment I realized he was never the guy I met that December; he was starting to feel like someone else. I was starting to see through the cracks in John's perfectly constructed mask more and more as time went on.

I put John and his buddy in my SUV and took his buddy home where John helped get him to his front door. John got back in the passenger seat silently and I drove us back to the trailer. I kept trying to ask him why he was upset, and he told me he does not like me being out at the bars, even though he was the one that took me. I was confused and stopped talking. Once he got out, I immediately locked the doors and he started screaming at me to get out of my SUV. I started crying and was going to drive off as soon as he was away from the tires, until he smashed his fist into my window. I still do not know how that window did not shatter. At that moment I could not have cared less if I accidentally ran over John's foot, so I chanced it and left. I did go to Sam's but when I got there I was sobbing, and he just led me to his couch where I passed out. As awful and deceitful as he could be, Sam would still offer shelter when I needed it.

The next morning, I had many texts from John asking where I was. I ignored him until roughly the 10th text and simply sent him a picture of the bruises he created on my left arm. He started text-sobbing and telling me he wanted to die; that he could not believe he grabbed me that hard. Sam spoke to me that morning in his kitchen like I was a friend and his only priority today was to make me forget about last night. We hopped in my SUV and drove about a half hour from our town. We walked around, had lunch, and talked about shallow things until I was ready to go confront John. That day, I felt that Sam and I could be friends. He was showing signs of wanting a friendship and not caring that I wanted to stay with John. I know now that I was very wrong.

I dropped Sam at home and drove to the trailer to talk to John. He was waiting for me in the living room and stood up calmly and quietly when I came in. The moment I set my purse down he came up and hugged me tight and started crying that he was sorry. I told him I forgave him and then I stressed that I needed a nap. When I woke up, I came out and John had an attitude that I remember very clearly because I immediately thought *you have no right to be the one upset after what you did.* When I asked him why he was upset, he said that I made up the whole event and he knows he would never do that. This is a classic example of gaslighting. This was becoming a trend with him that I was now starting to feel the effects of. I had finger-shaped bruises on my left arm that I silently raised up to his sight while staring at him annoyed. Then he told me I either did it to myself or I clearly fell on something. I was hurt, because even if I tried to do that to myself I wasn't able to line my right hand up with those marks. I was starting to feel more and more crazy. Again, the situation was dropped, and I was in the wrong at the end of the day.

Clearly, we were not doing well, and I was doing anything I could to spend all my time with friends lately. I could not do anything right by him and my self-worth was completely deteriorating. I would go out to have drinks or go over to my girlfriends houses and just stay there until I was tired enough to go home. John hated that I was never home, and I understood that, but I did not know how to leave him. I couldn't stand being around his false love any more than I had to. The accusations were being pulled out of thin air at this point. There was one day I was at my grandpa's when John texted me saying one of his friends got a picture of me dancing with some guy at a bar. I did not panic or try to fight with him because I knew for a fact that I never did that. Every single time I went out I had a ring I would put on my left hand and pretend I was engaged or married if I did have a man approach me. All of my girlfriends used to make fun of me for it and say it was sad and that he did not even deserve that much.

I got back home, and John was sitting on the couch, looking angry as ever. I told him to show me this picture that he claimed existed. He first told me, after already freaking out on me in text message, "Well, it's fuzzy and dark so now I don't know for sure." I just rolled my eyes and grabbed his phone. This picture was almost pitch-black. All I could make out was that there was a tall man, very shadowed, dancing with a woman my height, but definitely not my weight.

"I am flattered that you think I am that thin, but please look at that woman's left leg and tell me what you don't see," I said to him.

"She doesn't have a tattoo there," he said softly.

This was not the first time one of his friends had "reported back" to him about me. I saw his friends often when I was out! I would even say hello to most of them. I never had anything to hide when I was out, and that is a fact. My situation with Sam was something I am ashamed of, but when I was out of the house I never searched for another man. No matter what I did or how well I behaved when I was not home, he would either hear exactly where I was, or he would get fed a lie about where I was not.

I had made the decision to start college online around this time, and John was not the most supportive person about it. I did not want this life anymore. I was broke, dependent, and mentally weak and that was not someone I had ever been before. I was struggling and having to stay up extremely late most nights to complete my work because I had no time while John was awake. That was another thing I started to resent him for; letting me clean and cook and not sit down until he went to bed. As the next couple months went by, tension was starting to build between us and his buddy, just like it had at Blake's house. The space was just too small, and we all lived drastically different lifestyles. This place was a dump in my opinion so when John told the landlord we wanted out, he really just had to bring up the rotting floor and the mold and the fight was over; we were allowed to leave one month early. Honestly, we were not sure what was going to happen with us. I had tried to break it off about 5 times at this point and John would change for a few days. That would be enough to make me stay while he went right back to his habits. Regardless of our worries, we began the hunt for an apartment because clearly I was not going anywhere. After a couple days we did find a really nice place uptown on the strip and I felt like maybe if we lived alone together, something would change.

John's mom helped us move on an extremely hot night that summer. Due to the fact I had nightly requirements for school, we had to stay the night at his mom's because we did not have internet until the following day when we were fully moved in. His mom was always ridiculously accommodating, even with how rocky John and I were. We woke up in the morning and finished moving in, getting our utilities set up, and settling. I will be honest, it looked hopeful and I could see he felt at ease. Some time went by and I had not heard much from Sam, and I was okay with it even though we saw each other from a far at work. Then, one night I was blindsided by a rage-filled text from Sam telling me he deserved to have me, and John did not.

That text made me sick to my stomach. I told Sam I knew that he went back to his previous girlfriend and that it did not work out, so he was clearly falling back on me. I further explained that I was not okay with his possessive words towards me over time and that we were a mistake. He responded passively but in agreement, to leave me alone, drop it, and move on. I thought about my actions all the time. I hated the fact I let another man even get close to me while still being with John. I was miserable, but I was still in the wrong. I never stopped apologizing to John for that in later years.

Things were going okay at the new place. Nothing was changing as far as John making more time for me, and I found it was easier to just let it be. My tending to him got worse and I blame myself for it. We had gotten to a point where we did not even eat dinner together more than once or twice a week. I made dinner and I brought it to him in his game room, where I would return an hour later to get his dishes and clean up the kitchen. I would function on autopilot most of the time, but there were nights where I would cry while doing the dishes just praying he would come into the kitchen and make things better. I was making his lunch for work for some time now as well, but at the time I did not mind it until it became expected of me. He would not say he expected it – but he just stopped making his lunch, so I just kept doing it.

I decided to go out one night after a volleyball game I subbed in with my friend Liam, who I had known for about a year now from work. Our relationship was strictly platonic and still is to this day. We went to a favorite bar of ours to grab a few drinks as I did not want to be home any more than I had to be lately. To be honest, I had been playing for about 4 weeks now and on those Thursdays, I would tell John we were going out as a group so I could sit at my favorite local place and drink alone. Being as I was a smoker at the time and Liam rarely smoked, I stepped out back to have a cigarette alone. I was watching a beer pong game on the back patio when I heard a familiar voice say my name. My entire body clenched up and I turned around to see it was my ex-boyfriend from when I had enlisted in the Army back in 2013. Our relationship was brief and pointless with no important details other than the fact he cheated on me and I allowed us to remain somewhat friends. I am really more forgiving and lax than John wanted to admit.

"Hey," I said when he got close enough to me.

"Who are you here with?" he asked.

"My buddy, Liam. Not John, if that's what you were asking." I smirked. He hated John.

"Yeah, look there's something I need to tell you about John." he lit his cigarette.

I felt a pit open in my stomach when I saw the facial expression he was carrying. There was no smirk, just a small hint of sadness and nerves. Up until now, to my knowledge, John had not cheated on me. My ex explained to me that he and John had a mutual close friend that had been seeing this girl for many years. Apparently, John has reached out to her, drunk and persistent, to try and hook up with many times over the past couple years. John and I had been together for about 2 years now, so I hesitantly asked my ex when the last time he had reached out to her was. He told me about 2 months ago.

I burst into tears and found Liam inside the bar. I told him we needed to go, and we left in my SUV. I was sobbing telling Liam I knew that he was talking to other women, but I did not want to find out, not like that. Liam placed his hand on my shoulder and told me to try to relax and hoped that this was just a misunderstanding. I took Liam home and sped back to the apartment John and I shared. It must have been somewhere between midnight and 1AM when I came into the bedroom and quietly nudged John telling him to get up. Once he was up I asked him who this girl was. In his defense, he was woken from a dead sleep and was disoriented. However, after I started crying and accusing him of what my ex told me, he got loud and angry.

"GET OUT. I can't believe how stupid you are!" he screamed at me while pointing to the door.

I froze for a moment because even to this day, no one ever saw the side of John I did. He was so angry and manipulative that in this moment, I almost felt like I was at fault for his actions. I ran into the game room where my closet was and packed a few outfits through the tears and nausea from the adrenalin. I called my grandpa and asked if I could come there while John was screaming at me in the background. To my surprise he answered his phone and unlocked his door for when I arrived. I ran inside and ran into my grandpa's arms sobbing in the dramatics of an alcohol-fueled and accusation-driven blowout. I went downstairs and laid in bed trying to force myself to get the 4 hours of sleep I had available before I had to get up and go to work. The moment my head hit the pillow, my phone was exploding with texts apologizing and asking where I was. After about 20 texts and 5 missed calls I responded saying I was at my grandpa's and to leave me alone.

The morning came and I managed to get about 3 hours of sleep. I called into work because I was shaking with anxiety from the night before. Looking back on these events, I feel like I was in a hell of my own making. How was I supposed to go home and be angry at John when I had also tried to find attention from someone else? It was different to me in the sense that I tried so hard to get his attention and please him and he still tried to talk to someone else. It made me feel slightly less guilty about my few months of hiding my conversations with another man, but it still would not be right of me to go home and beat him down.

John went to work that day, so I took my things I had brought to my grandpa's and went home. Once John got home, he told me his version of the truth. He claimed that a long time ago he had a chance to be with this girl, but he treated her badly and lost his chance. He went on to explain that sometimes when he gets drunk, he just wants to apologize to her. I did not believe him, but I said I did, and I dropped it. The following week John had a basketball game at the high school with other people from his graduating class. I was not incredibly interested in watching grown men play basketball unprofessionally, but all jokes aside, it was a fun time and a good excuse to hang out with his mom and niece.

I was in the bleachers with the girls when I got a text from my ex with more information about the situation he had informed me of at the bar the previous week. Because I knew this was just the beginning of John's lies, I did not want this information. I did not ask for it. My stomach dropped and my eyes filled with tears. I did not hesitate to pass the phone to John's mom, and she also started to tear up. She did not say anything, but her eyes were apologetic. I ran outside and called my ex because I did not want to have to wait for even 2 seconds for my questions to be answered. I hung up with him and got the phone number of the boyfriend of this woman.

I then texted him and asked him if this was all true while apologizing for bringing up any drama. He told me it was all true.

I waited in John's car until the game ended. He entered the car and could tell something was wrong, so on the drive home I explained what I had found out. He was bright red in the face and yelling at me that I was bringing this up again.

"So, this is all my fault, like everything else right?" I cried at him.

"You will do anything to start a fight so yeah, this is not what you think." He muttered.

Once we got home, we shut the door and let it rip. He was screaming at me to stop crying and I was begging him to tell me why I have never been enough for him. I remember quietly asking him why he would not just let me go the times I had tried to leave. He laughed and said I was crazy. At that moment, the word crazy felt like a punch in the face. I called my ex, and then 3-wayed the boyfriend of this girl. This man that John used to be friends with is a decent guy, and years later I can see clearly why he had not contacted John in years. They all spoke on speaker phone while John was told that he needed to stop contacting this girl and that I did not deserve the lies about it. John then attacked my ex for telling me and accused him of trying to get me back, which was a joke. My ex was an equally large pile of garbage.

Once the call ended, I ran to the back porch and smoked alone for about 20 minutes. John was storming about inside on his phone, texting God knows who about what just happened. When I came back inside I washed my hands like I usually did after smoking and I sat on the couch contemplating what to do next. John came and sat by me and did not say a word. Within seconds his hands were all over me. This was John's typical last resort when he had nothing left for defense; he would initiate intimacy of some sort. I always fell for it, and that was always his way to get me to move on from something without having a much-needed discussion.

This blowout was the last major fight we had for a little while. I knew John was talking to women while gaming, and I had only found one incriminating conversation from him so far on his Xbox, so I did not even know how to address the situation. To this day he does not know what I found, and I never brought it up. Things coasted how they always had been, and I just adapted to the fact that this was my life now. At one point at the end of August of 2015, we had even discussed trying to get pregnant. How ignorant I feel now thinking that a baby would bring us closer together. This was the man that discarded me so quickly at the beginning with the miscarriage and I thought bringing an innocent little person into this mix was going to be a good thing. We tried on and off for a few weeks, until one of the worst nights of my life happened.

Blake and Lana were going out drinking on a night in October, and at this point John and Blake had made up for all the issues that happened while we all lived together and got past it. We all gathered to pre-game at Blake and Lana's house before heading downtown to the bars. Everything was going fine, and we all split into groups as usual and loaded into cabs out front of the house. I sat in John's lap and was having a great time with him for the first time in a while. He had his hand around my waist, and we were laughing with our friends. It really felt like this was going to be a simple fun night out. But even in that moment, it felt like we were just actors in a play and our masks would fall off soon, so why get excited. I know vivid details of this night because of how horrific it was.

We got to the first bar and it was just me, Lana, Blake, and John. We were having a great time listening to music, taking photos, and having drinks. I needed a cigarette and John did not smoke, in fact he hated that I did, but he said he wanted to come outside with me. I agreed and we went out back where we were greeted with an empty patio. This conversation seems meaningless, but it always stuck with me.

"You are so different from other girls I've been with," he said, putting his arm around me.

"What like how I look?" I laughed and lit my cigarette.

"Yeah, before you I just had 1 serious relationship, but any other girls I've hooked up with don't look like you." He said, "My one ex I have was crazy. Most of the girls I've hooked up with are." That statement instantly made me angry, as it does not take a genius to know that's improbable.

"What are you trying to say?" I asked, not really wanting an answer.

"I just always wanted to try out the Goth or punk looking girls, with tattoos and the piercings, you're just different than the rest that's all." He laughed.

I did feel pretty in that moment with him. It was a strange statement and I do not think he meant I was

30

this treasure, but that I was a phase to try. This statement should have had the opposite effect on me. I cannot put words in his mouth or thoughts in his head, so I cannot say what he meant. Sometimes a cigar is just a cigar. We went back inside where we drank a lot more. I started to worry because we both changed when we drank. If I drank too much, I got sad, but I stayed rational. If he drank too much, he got mean, and lost all sense of reason. Lana and Blake wanted to hit a different bar at this point, so we all went outside and started walking. When we got to the next bar, the final bar, is when it started.

When we were walking into the bar, some girl was all over John. You know the type: high-pitched squeal when she saw him and ran to give him an overly dramatic hug that lasted way too long. I honestly believe he did not see it that way and just saw it as a hug, but this girl tossed herself at him. I immediately got upset at her, but John thought I was angry at him and I cannot say he was wrong in assuming that. Lana saw me glaring at him for what just happened, and she took me to the bar and told me to let it go. I was standing at the bar when I glanced back hoping John would be coming over to me. What I saw shook me to my core. You see, a while back I told Lana that I was thinking about really leaving John and that I had met Sam and really liked him. This was all before I realized Sam was crazy and that I had a deeply rooted need to stay with John. Lana said she would never say a word, but to this day I know I put her in a bad spot asking that secrecy of her.

When I turned around to find John, Blake was whispering into his ear looking profoundly serious, and John's head slowly turned toward me with a look in his eyes that I still cannot match an emotion to. I knew in that moment that Lana had told Blake, and Blake just told John. Time seemed to stop for a moment. The music felt like a faint humming in a distance, and my face felt hot from all the blood rushing to my head. I was instantly sober. John started to head for the front door, and I ran to catch him. Once we were both outside he confronted me.

"Sam – really! How long?" he screamed in front of strangers.

"Please let me explain, it's not what you think." I tried to plead with him.

He refused to listen to me. He was right to be angry, I just hated that this was the time and place that this was brought into light. I had planned to tell him in a way that would be private and not hurt him this suddenly. My heart sped up as he looked at my face with what appeared to be a mix of anger, betrayal, and confusion. I panicked and I started sprinting through all the strangers on the sidewalk to get to my SUV. I heard him yelling after me, but I could not stop running. I've wondered a few times over the years what the outcome might have been if I had turned around at his call. This was another incident where I felt like I was insane. I was miserable and I knew that he would never treat me better, but any time we got close to breaking up, we both felt like we were going to die. This addiction was worse than anything I have ever experienced, and I was at a point where I needed it to stop at any cost.

I drove to a nearby store and bought razors because all I could think about was my shame and my heart feeling shattered because of something I did, not him. I got back in my car and drove towards Chicago. It was about 12:30 or 1AM and I told myself, if you can stop crying in the next hour, turn around and drive home. I called Sam and told him what had happened and that I was sorry to him as well. He listened and tried to calm me down, but I heard his ex in the background asking who he was talking to. I had caused enough damage at this point, so I hung up. I pulled over in a small town and parked my SUV. I curled up in my front seat and hurt my arm pretty badly.

At that moment, I got a text from my little sister. She did not know what had happened, and it was way past her bedtime, but there it was; a text randomly telling me she loved me. That was my sign that this was not the right way out. I wrapped my arm up in my sweater and drove towards home. I called John and he answered telling me that he had walked home immediately in the rain alone. This was miles from our apartment, but clearly he was upset and needed to be alone. I told him what I did, and he told me to come home. I returned to the apartment at 3AM roughly, wrapped my arm in napkins, and laid on the couch until I passed out. The following morning was a Sunday, and I awoke to him sitting in the recliner next to the couch gaming. This grief had a gravity that felt so heavy in that moment that I thought it was capable of taking my ability to breathe away.

I sat up and asked if I should start packing my things. John said no, and asked me how far things had gone with Sam. I told him the truth and asked him if he had talked to Sam last night. John told me he called Sam and confronted him. Sam told John that I did not deserve some of the things he had done to me, how miserable I was, and that he would leave me alone. Sam also told John that he needed to forgive me. I would not have believed this coming out of Sam's mouth, but considering John said it, even with hate in his voice, I knew it was true.

"Do you? Can you forgive this?" I asked him.

"It will take time, but I don't want you to leave." He paused looking at my arm. "We are going to the hospital." He stated, firmly.

I was scared to go because I did not know how to lie to a doctor's face to keep from being put on suicide watch and missing work. However, the doctor and I had spoken privately, and I told him how stupid this was and that I am not at risk. He believed me and after stitching me up, he released me into John's care. I was not sure if it would be worse to stay or just take this as a sign that I needed to leave. I honestly believe in my heart that I could not have forgiven John if I knew for a fact that he touched another woman, and I did not know why he was going to try to forgive me. Part of me believed, and still does, that it was never about Sam to me. I wonder if subconsciously I was trying to force myself into a situation where John had to make the choice to break things off, because I simply could not. As I sat on our couch next to John that Sunday evening I felt a strong fog in the air around us. There was a grey area I was lingering in wondering if we would make it past this event. Did I want to make it past this? Did he? I was vibrating with anxiety the entire evening as I tried to make conversation.

"Do you want dinner?" I asked.

"I'm not really hungry," he said softly, without breaking gaze with the TV.

I slipped into bed that night asking God what I was supposed to do next. I knew I had messed up, but I knew I did what I did for a reason. John wrapped his arm over my stomach and said goodnight. That was it. That was the period in our chapter that I knew would be used against me for the rest of this relationship. That *goodnight* felt like a cloaked *you will not live this down.*

And I did not live it down.

Christmas was around the corner at this point, and I was in charge of getting gifts for everyone. By everyone, I mean up until being with me John did not get gifts for his family. Birthdays, Christmas, or any other holidays were now my thing and I did not really mind it. I love nothing more than getting gifts for people, and now I got to do it for my family and his. We had Christmas at his mom's house like we usually did. I enjoyed any events we had at his mom's because of how kind his family was towards me. The holidays were about the only peaceful times I could count on in this relationship.

New Years Eve was never a big celebration with John and me. We would try to stay up till midnight to watch the ball drop on TV, but this was the 3rd year we had watched it together and it felt like it lost its magic on us. The first time was in 2013 the December that I had met him, and that was fun to do together because we had just met, and it felt romantic. But, as the years went on we just did not get excited about it anymore. John went into his game room and I watched TV until we went to bed. This anti-climatic holiday brought our 2nd year together to a quiet end.

Chapter Three
Trapped

I took a break from drinking at this point along with doing anything other than being home. This was when I met one of my best friends at work, Melanie. We became awfully close over a few short months and I started to open up to her about my current situation. It was hard to believe we had entered the year of 2016 already. Things were going alright with John and we promised each other we would try to put more effort into doing things outside of the apartment together. John and I had a few good memories, inside jokes, and good times together throughout our relationship. There were stupid noises we would make at each other that made the other one laugh, but made us look stupid in public, which we loved. It was like constantly letting your phone battery reach 2%, then charging it until it got to 10%, and repeating the cycle. The good times were nowhere near enough for me, yet I let them be my signs to stay. I also got along with his family well, to the point I felt like I would be a part of it someday. John got along with my siblings and other family members we would see occasionally throughout the year from out-of-town as well. I will say that my parents never loved him, and I feel that was because I was constantly upset about whatever fight we were having that week. Things would switch up so quickly with us that it was like whiplash.

We could be having a decent time and if we were around his friends, all bets were off. If we were around my friends, I could not avoid angering him. There just never seemed to be reciprocation on his end when I wanted anything, like if I was tired and wanted to go home: we were not going home. If he wanted to leave early and I wanted to stay we were going home, or I could stay the night somewhere else. There was one night where I brought him out with a girl I had met at work and her boyfriend. We just decided to go to one bar that we were all familiar with. I'm not sure how long we were there, but if I had to guess I would say about an hour before John told me he was done and ready to go home. I was surprised because it seemed like he was having a good time, but he looked irritated. I told him I wanted to stay with my friend and would just get a cab home and he could leave. He took my wrist, smiled at my friends, and said we were leaving. He led me back to his car and we both sat inside arguing.

"Why, John? Why won't you ever let me stay and have fun on my own time?" I cried.

"Because it's time to go home, we have been here long enough," he said, as he started the car.

"You know what – no. I am staying let me out," I said, as I exited his car.

"Are you kidding me?" he said. He always said this when he had nothing else to say.

I walked away. I turned back at him, waved aggressively, and walked away as I watched him slam his door and drive off.

I have read many books, articles, blogs, and life stories of men and women who have escaped narcissistic abuse, neglect, gaslighting, and psychopathic environments that had no idea what they were neck deep in until they escaped. The sad part is, I still have nightmares occasionally where I hear him telling me I was a psycho. I wake up after re-living certain arguments or nights where he would leave me in a puddle of tears on the floor that felt as deep as the ocean. I used to care that I left feeling like I died, and he was going to tell everyone he was the hero in this story and that he dodged a bullet. I am to a point now that I am okay with his new supply thinking I was the crazy one, and I hope she is not dealing with what I did. Sadly, we all know grown people do not change, they just do not. Today, that is not in my mind. John claimed he was surprised every single time I tried to leave or explain I was unhappy, like he never saw the signs.

I gave *so* many signs, and I gave them all the time. Looking back I can say with certainty that there was always a small part of me fighting in the back of my mind wanting to stand up, wipe my own tears away, and say *I don't need this, and I don't need you. You are the one that needs me.* I have dreamt about closure, revenge, and wanting him to suffer. The thing about finding peace and rebuilding your life the right way, is that those feelings melt away. I realized that I was just his mother, in a sense. I fixed his problems, I cleaned, I cooked, I budgeted, and really any other responsibility someone could possibly take from someone. I remember being in shock the day I had to show a grown man how to write a check. So no, I am not surprised he thought he was in love with me. I am surprised he was too much of a coward to ever give me a real apology prior to me trying to walk out the door.

We were trying to heal at this point after what had happened. I had found out he had attempted to cheat on me multiple times, and he and he had found out about Sam. We were both attempting to keep our relationship afloat in our own way. I was staying home every possible minute of the day, and he was doing exactly what he had always done; gamed and slept. I was getting desperate to get his affection more than ever, and the only thing I could think of was doing something crazy for his birthday, so I did. It was June, and I contacted Blake and asked him if I could throw a surprise party for John at his house. Blake was so excited and said yes immediately. I had a two-tear cake made with the Jordan logo on it and the number 25, for his 25th birthday. I went over to Blake's and decorated the lower-level and put the cake in the fridge. At this point in time, neither John nor myself had a Facebook. We decided we had enough inter-relationship issues that we did not need to involve the rest of the world's opinion on if we were still together or not. After saying that, I feel it's sadder to me now than it was at the time. Anyway, due to the fact we did not have a social media platform for me to massively invite people, Blake said he would take care of it.

John's birthday weekend came, and I told him that Blake wanted to hangout before we went to dinner. John seemed suspicious but he agreed. Blake pulled everything off perfectly. He made sure everyone parked down the street from his house so that John would not see everyone's cars. We entered the house and Blake was so convincing that he was just walking around upstairs brushing his teeth casually. John was laughing asking what Blake had been up to. I knew he was thinking about getting a new pool table but had not done it yet. So, I said we should go down and see his new purchase. That seemed like an easy way to get John downstairs. Blake put on a shirt and led us downstairs where John was greeted with a massive surprise. He lit up and was so happy to see his friends and family as the music started.

I felt so happy because I had caused that smile. We all laughed and partied for a few hours to celebrate John. As the night went on, only friends remained. Those friends wanted to get crazy and then go out to the bars. I had hoped that would not be the case, but I was prepared for it. I watched John go into his cousin's back room with his buddy that always had cocaine on him, so I knew what he was back there doing. I let it go and waited for them to come back out so we could go downtown. I stopped drinking because I knew John would get drunk tonight and I needed to make sure we got home. Once we all got cabs and arrived downtown, it did not take long for the inevitable to happen.

I continued to drink water at the first bar we went to because I did not want to be drunk at the same time as John. After everyone got bored of this bar, we decided to leave and go to another one down a few blocks from where we were at. Things were not going to bad at this point and I was happy that we were only about an hour from bar close. John was absolutely hammered, and I told him it would be a good idea to go home. He actually nodded and pointed to the bathroom. I laughed and said go ahead I will wait outside the door since he was stumbling. I was leaning up against one side of the hallway outside of the bathrooms and when I saw John come out and start walking back down the hallway, this girl wrapped her arm around his neck, put her leg up on his hip, and got way too close to his face for my comfort. John just stood there and smiled at her. The rage that filled my body was not even for John; it was for this woman. This was the second time, with a totally different woman, where this had happened right in front of me. I could only imagine what happened when I was not around to see it. I grabbed the back of her shirt and told her to back up. She just smirked and walked away as I tried to kill John with my eyes. He was so drunk at this point that his eyes were fluttering to stay open. His older sister was with us that night, so I found her and asked her to take us home. She managed to pile John into her car and started driving us to our apartment.

We came up to a stop sign one block away from home, and John jumped out of the car and started staggering home. I told his sister to just make the turn and park in our parking lot. She asked if I needed her help, but I told her no. I got John inside and led him to the bathroom. He was leaning over the toilet gagging and crying that he did not want to throw up. Looking at him like this, I decided that I would wait until morning to tell him I was angry about the past hour of the night. I was getting nervous that he was acting so sick still an hour after hanging over the toilet. I called his mom and told her I wanted to be safe and have her come check him out in case he had alcohol poisoning. She was there within 5 minutes, jumping onto our back deck to avoid the locked front doors, and I was cracking up watching her barreling through the back yard. I know she hates me now, but I really loved that woman.

She came inside and checked on John in the bathroom. He was still crying that he did not want to throw up, so she kept trying to convince him to crawl to the bedroom and lie down. After about an hour of us trying to get him to bed, he finally made the crawl and passed out. John's mom stayed on the couch that night until morning just in case he really had drank too much.

"How much did he drink?" She whispered to me in the living room.

"Well, I stopped counting before we even arrived downtown," I said, rolling my eyes.

"Anything else?" She asked.

I just stared at her with a facial expression that hinted towards *what do you think.*

"Got it." She said, "Thanks for the blanket and pillow, I'll leave early and try to be quiet."

She left around 830AM and woke me up to let me know she was happy I had called her. John woke up at about 10AM and I told him what had happened with the woman at the bar. He told me he was really sorry and that if he were sober he would have told her to back up.

"So, if you're drunk it's okay?" I asked him annoyed.

"Well I wasn't in my right mind I said I'm sorry." He snapped back at me.

"Whatever. I don't care if it's your birthday John, you can't get that drunk if you're going to let women drape themselves over you," I said getting angrier.

I grabbed my purse and told John I had to go get toilet paper, and I left. When I returned home, John said that he asked two of his friends that were with us about the woman I told him about. They both told him they were at the front of the bar but never saw him with a woman. So of course, I was again a liar that made up the whole thing. I remember throwing the toilet paper at the ground and calling him a few names before I left and went to my girlfriend's house for a few hours. I cannot put into words, even years later, what was happening in my mind anymore. Every single event, fight, accusation, lie, and near-breakup made me think twice about everything I did. I was beginning to drink more, overanalyze everything he did, and started to lose interest in things that I used to love. I hadn't painted in months, and that was not like me.

Sometimes the day would end, and I would realize that the only thing I had been looking forward to all day was going to bed. After the whole Sam fiasco, I had seen a mental health specialist and been put on depression and anxiety medication. I did everything I could the past couple years to fight my mind hard enough to not be put on anything and just fight through it. Looking back, I realize that there is nothing wrong with getting help and being on medication; that's why those resources exist. John did not love that I got put on those medications for the simple fact that he hated pills, but he still acted hopeful that my depression that "came out of nowhere" was going to be taken care of. I was also smoking more now than I ever had and I could not seem to cut back even if I tried.

This was about the time I had found out my parents were going to be moving away. My stepfather was being relocated for work and my mom had called me over one night to tell me in person. When I got to their apartment, she was waiting outside for me on the steps. I sat down and she explained what was happening, and my heart started to feel really heavy. The only family I had here was my parents and sisters, and my grandparents. My mom and my grandpa were always my safe places, and I never dreamt of a time in the near future where I would be so far from either of them. My mom told me they would be moving to Minnesota soon and she was not sure for how long.

I did not cry when she told me because I knew how sad she was, and I did not want to make it harder on her. I got in my car to drive home and completely fell apart. Luckily, our apartment was only 2 minutes from my mom's. When I got home, I came inside crying audibly and hard. John barely looked away from the TV for more than 2 seconds to look at me.

"What's wrong?" He asked

"My parents are moving away; I don't know how I am going to be able to live this far from my mom John." I started crying harder.

I had only made it into the living room and just past the couch before I knelt on the floor and continued to cry. He told me, after a couple minutes of me crying to myself, to give him until the end of his game and he would be able to concentrate on what I was saying. When he said that I instantly stopped crying and stared at him disgusted.

"Are you kidding me? I am on the floor sobbing and you can't get up from your stupid game for a minute?" I cried.

"Wow relax I said give me a minute," he said, annoyed.

I ran into the bathroom, locked the door, and finished having my moment. Once I got myself together and realized this was just a sad change, but not the end of the world, I went to bed. John came in and tried to talk to me, but I pretended I was asleep until he left the room. He did this all of the time when I needed him. He could never just come be with me if he was gaming, watching football, or out with his friends. If I needed him, it had better be when he's not busy with something else. Nowadays, I honestly believed that I was a burden in his eyes. Not on anyone else in my life, just John. I hated how I looked anymore, because clearly I was not attractive enough to warrant attention from him. All I knew was that I was intelligent and was going to graduate, no matter what.

Fall was upon us after a couple months of me doing nothing but focusing on my schoolwork and trying to keep the fights to a minimum at home. I was set to graduate soon and being honest, I had been white knuckling my way through my tests and assignments for months. Even on nights where I was being given the cold shoulder, or John got angry at me and went out with his buddies, I would sit at the computer and cry, alone, while I finished my work. To this day I still do not know how I did not fail or drop out. I heard John brag about my schooling and my job progress to people all of the time in public, but I can count on one hand how many times in private he ever told me he was proud of me or asked how classes were going.

Work was going really well for me; I had recently been promoted to one of the best teams of people I've ever worked with. I still have so many friends I stayed in touch with at this job because they were just a different type of people. Even some of my supervisors and leads from this place were pillars in my life and held my hand through really rough times at home and are still my close friends today. My schedule changed when I got promoted and I was now working until 5PM instead of 330PM like before. I loved getting off at 330 because it was easier to make appointments and go to the gym. However, considering that my home-life was 80% fighting and silent treatments, I liked leaving work later.

In October of 2016 is another memory I try to relive as little as possible. I love Halloween, it's my second favorite holiday, and up until meeting John I have always dressed up and participated in some way. Halloween of 2014 I had asked to dress up and maybe go do something – but John agreed that all he would do was go to a pumpkin patch. I had taken him up on that offer and for the most part it was a decent time with my family as well. In 2015 for Halloween I was allowed to put up decorations, but he refused to dress up or go anywhere, like the haunted forest or to a costume party. This year I begged him to dress up and maybe go out to the bars with some friends. He said there was absolutely no way he would do either one of those things. Of course, this ended up starting a fight with us because something that he saw as little, I had been trying to get out of him for 3 Halloweens now.

I realized that I was in fact allowed to leave and find other plans, so I asked Melanie if I could come out to her parents bar and maybe we could dress up together. This bar was out in Wisconsin and it was not on any obnoxious strips, but it did get busy some nights. I loved having drinks with Melanie at the bar because I did not know anyone else out there and I felt no one was keeping their eye on me. Melanie agreed happily and we met up at the costume store to mess around and find something we could wear together. We ended up landing on cop costumes, and if I'm being honest they were a bit flashy and everything I usually make fun of women for wearing, but this year I just did not care. I came home that afternoon from shopping and told John that I had bought a costume and I would be spending Friday night at the bar with Melanie. John said he'd prefer I stayed home, but he knew that got him out of any more arguing about his presence, so he did not fight with me much on me going out for once.

Even though John had reluctantly agreed to let me go out, when I put on the costume and started getting ready he was immediately upset. This costume was about 3 inches above knee length, had short sleeves, no cleavage, but was tight. It was absolutely nowhere near the most showing costume I've ever seen, but I was being judged at that moment by a man that would question me every time I put makeup on to leave the house. I cannot count how many times I would hear, "Who are you so dressed up for?" when I would literally just be in jeans and have my hair straightened.

"I showed you the costume earlier, so why is it now that you have an issue?" I asked. "Would you prefer I wear leggings or something?

"Because you look kind of slutty and are going to get hit on," he said.

"Well I'm in control of how I respond to that if it happens, but I just want to drink with Melanie," I said, already deflated. "If you're worried then come with me."

"Whatever." He scoffed.

I left that night and drove out to the bar. When I got there, I was one of about 5 people and Melanie was behind the bar not in costume. I yelled at her playfully until she put it on and returned to bartend. We had such a good time and were laughing so hard our sides hurt. I did not feel stressed, or watched, or judged by anyone. I was surrounded by my good friends and I ended up exceeding the time John wanted me home. I had a few too many drinks, and I realized I needed to leave. I should not have driven that night, but I knew that John was going to yell at me for being gone as long as I was. When I arrived at the apartment, John was already asleep, so I changed and got into bed. The next morning, I woke up and went about things as I usually do; I made breakfast and asked John how his night was. He said it was fine and asked what I did and why I was gone so late. I told him that I was having a good time and just lost track. John told me that it is obnoxious and disrespectful for me to not stick to my original plan of when I would be home. I think this was the point I realized he was trying to enforce curfews with me. I just stared at him and did not respond.

We had recently bought a new TV; I think it was one of the 4k ones with the insane color clarity. I want to say we had gotten the TV about a week or two ago and it stopped working, so we had scheduled to have a repair man come to the apartment today and take a look at it. They are so high-tech now that when I called, they asked for a number on the back of the TV and they could instantly see the motherboard was fried. We were expecting the repair man any time now, and John was about to pass me headed towards the bathroom when I told him that I could not handle how he makes me feel when I try to have a life outside of the apartment.

He instantly got annoyed and brought up what had happened last year and told me he would not be surprised if I was out with my other boyfriend (Sam) last night. We stood there and he yelled at me for a bit as I held back tears. I hated when he got that loud. He would look at me and smirk as he got louder and louder. Accusations would start flying out of nowhere. One time he accused me of going home with someone on a night that I was home with the flu, and he was out drinking. He claimed he just mixed up the date, but his entire explanation made absolutely no sense. Just then, there was a knock at our door, and we knew it was the repair man. I ran to the bathroom to clean up my face and let John get the door. Once I came out of the bathroom, I got dressed in the bedroom and put sunglasses on so the repair man would not misread my puffy eyes.

"John I have to run some errands and am probably going to Melanie's." I muttered.

"Yeah." He glared at me clearly wanting to stop me but could not in present company.

I arrived at Melanie's and told her about everything that had happened. When I was with Melanie some of that fog always lifted. We continued our visit for hours before texts started between John and me. He was angry at first, and then started begging me to come home. I was scared to go home, not because I thought he would hurt me, but because if I went home the fog would return and I would show him that I was okay with unresolved issues being ignored. After he finally grasped that I wasn't coming home, he got more and more angry. I said some things I should not have said about how I knew he was talking to other women and that he should just go out and bring one of them home.

He finally turned his approach around and told me that he did not want to sit home in his own tears and was going out with Blake and his friends. His own tears. Going out now that I'm not home. I did not know which statement angered me more. The amount of times I would be sobbing on my knees on the floor while he neglected me, tormented me, left me, and made me feel invisible were countless at this point. But now he was *sitting with his tears* because I did not want to come home and play this game right now. The fact that now he was going to go out without me right after telling me recently that it was inappropriate for me to go out alone filled me with rage. What was

51

happening? Did he make this situation explode this much so that he had an excuse to not only go out without me, but also make me out to be the one feeling guilty at the end of the day? I stepped outside to Melanie's porch to have a cigarette and organize my thoughts. On one hand, I wanted him to go out without me and sadly I had hoped that maybe he would actually miss me. On the other hand, I knew who he was, and I was scared he would intentionally get into some sort of trouble.

I told him I really needed him to leave me alone and I stopped responding to him. A few hours went by and I started to get worried about what he would do to retaliate, because that was how John operated. I could not get a response after about 3 texts in those 2 hours. I nervously drove home and was greeted with an empty apartment. I checked every room to make sure he really was not home. When I entered the game room, something took over me and I collapsed to the floor. I was so angry and confused anymore that I did not even know how to appropriately react to situations. I called Melanie to tell her he was gone and that I did not want to be here alone and asked if I should go look for him or leave him be. She told me that if I did not get back in my SUV and come back to her house she would send her husband to pick me up. She always made sure I was okay, no matter what. I agreed and said to give me a few minutes and I would head back. The silence in that apartment was deafening, so I got up and left. I climbed in my SUV and drove back to Melanie's where I slept on the couch.

When I woke up, I had a text from John's phone, but his mother had written it. The text said that he was home and that she had found him the night before. I hated that she texted me from his phone because that meant she had seen all of the things we had said to each other, and I could not undo that. I got off of Melanie's couch and gathered all of my things to head home. When I got to the apartment, John's mom was gone but he was still in bed. I entered the bedroom and asked what his mom meant by "found him". He went on to explain to me that he and Blake had gone to, what I can only explain as a trap house, with extremely shady people the night before. He said that he was so upset he did a bunch of coke and started walking home. His mother informed me moments prior in a text that she found him shirtless on the sidewalk lying down.

I had no words for what he had just told me. Our fight was rough, but there was no excuse for what he did. I know that if he was with who he said he was with; he did things I did not even want to know about.

"I stayed out later than I originally planned to, but we just needed time away from each other," I said, softly.

"If you hadn't told me to bring home another woman I wouldn't have even gone out." He snapped back at me.

"I know you're talking to other women, serious or not, and it just came out in an ugly tone. I'm sorry I said what I said." I snapped, feeling my eyes fill with tears. "So, did you find a woman last night?" I asked.

"I don't remember half of last night but clearly I didn't bring anyone home," he said, annoyed.

"Well clearly, considering your mother had to find you downtown shirtless on a sidewalk," I said, as I started to walk away. "Just another thing for us to forget about, right?" I was fully crying at this point.

"Do you even want to be with me anymore?" he asked, sounding choked up.

"Don't you dare. You only cry when you know you're in the wrong." I raised my voice. "I love you and you treat me like garbage, you have people monitoring me, and you don't trust me, what am I supposed to do?" at this point I was sobbing.

He did not respond for what seemed like an eternity, but after a few minutes he told me that he would be better, and this would never happen again. Sadly, by this stage in our relationship, I could tell when he was forcing tears. So, I watched his eyes twitch and he let out a single tear, because he knew that was all it took for me. He won. He always won, and the whole situation was dropped.

The holidays were the same as they always were; John and I put aside our arguments, contempt, and misery for those last two months of the year. I believe that Thanksgiving and Christmas were a joy that we shared, and that is why we would both do everything in our power to not fight during the holidays. We had Christmas at his moms as usual, and then later in the day we stopped by my grandparent's house to say hi and exchange gifts. It's in these two brief months that we are happy, distracted, and without stress. That is not a good thing, it sounds sweet and spiritual, but it was not. No relationship should be seasonal. Our bond was built on games, confusing addiction for misery, and worst of all: knowing it would come to an end and doing everything we could to prolong it.

Chapter Four
Deteriorating

We are now in January of 2017; things seemed to be improving. John had been paying a lot of attention to me lately. I stress *seemed to be improving*. He was asking me about school occasionally and he even made dinner recently. It was decent, so I was almost annoyed that he had cooked for us about 7 times in the 3 years we had been together. John and I started to agree that the apartment was way too small for us. The sad part of our next chapter is that even though I knew some part of me really needed to leave; I was still hanging onto the idea of a future with him by my fingertips. I was at the point where being awake was physically painful because I was constantly sick to my stomach. My anxiety medication was hardly working anymore, and that was really scaring me.

My birthday was coming up and usually, John would take me out to dinner or get me a card. On my 22nd birthday he did absolutely nothing except say, "Happy Birthday" via text the morning of. The following day he got me a card that said, "Sorry I suck and didn't do anything for you." That was next to a pack of some candy I liked. I know he did this because one of my girlfriends gave him grief about not doing anything for me. This year his mom asked me if I would be cool with all of us going to one of my favorite restaurants. I said absolutely and was incredibly happy I would be spending the evening with them. The day of my birthday was normal, I went to work then came home to shower and get ready for dinner. After I showered and was almost done getting ready, John came into the living room and sat me down on the couch.

"I want to give you something, but you need to understand it first," he said.

"Okay, why?" I asked, very eager to see what he was holding behind his back.

"This is not an engagement ring; I am not asking you to marry me. This is just a promise that I will at some point, okay?" He held the ring out in front of him facing me.

The ring was a small square diamond with a silver band. It was a pretty ring, even though it was not my taste at all. There were a lot of emotions washing over me in this moment. On one hand, this was a ring from John to me and it had to mean he loved me, right? On the other hand, he just made it extremely clear that marriage was still really not even on the table after over 3 years together. I smiled and took the box from him.

"Can I put it on?" I smiled.

"Of course," he said, smiling back, "But wear it on your right hand." He requested.

"Doesn't it go on my left hand?" I asked, kind of sad.

"Just wear it on your right hand please." he said, sounding annoyed.

"Okay, well thank you," I said, feeling a bit deflated.

We went to dinner that night and John immediately had me show his mother and siblings the ring. Everyone thought it was very pretty, but I felt a want to take it off. We all ate dinner and talked about our days. About an hour passed and we waved the waitress down for our bill so we could go home. On the drive home, I kept twisting the ring on my finger and John noticed. He asked if it did not fit, and I told him it did and that I was just fidgety. We arrived home and got ready for bed. I knew that since I had gotten a diamond ring and had my dinner paid for, that John was going to try and be intimate tonight, so I took my time getting ready for bed. After lying in bed for a moment, John actually did not try anything and said goodnight. I was relieved, not because I did not want to feel loved by him even in his most shallow way, but I felt really sad and just did not want to have to hide it anymore. What a birthday.

The worst memory I have involving that ring was one night towards the end of spring when I stayed to late at Melanie's. We had been visiting and it was going on midnight, so I told John I wanted to stay the night. He was furious and I cannot remember why exactly but he said that he was done with my inconsistencies not arriving home on time. I just shut my phone off and went to bed. After all, he knew where I was and what I was doing, and I had done nothing wrong. When I got up in the morning and turned my phone back on, I had a handful of messages from John. They did not say anything important and were really just passive aggressive stabs at me. I returned home mid-morning and entered the apartment quietly in case he was still sleeping. It was completely silent other than the fan in the bedroom. I had put the ring in its case the night before and left it on the coffee table because the whole reason I had gone to Melanie's was to paint with her daughter and I knew I would either get it dirty or lose it. Other than that moment, I did not take it off – even to shower. I told John exactly why I was taking it off and where I was placing it.

The ring was no longer on the table. I looked around in every room in the apartment and I could not find it. I finally went into the bedroom and woke John up to ask him where the ring was. He slowly opened his eyes and told me that he was going to hold onto it until I deserved it again. I did not move for about 2 minutes when he said that. This man had given me a ring while chanting a speech of anti-commitment, and then made sure I would not wear it on my left hand because someone might think he actually wanted to stay with me. Then, I upset him and had the ring confiscated because I did not follow his rules. It took me a week of being silent and agreeable to get the ring back, but no apology came with it.

It was May and my graduation was around the corner, actually it was next weekend to be exact. I was so excited that I had accomplished something and that my classes were finally over. I never said this out loud, but my biggest internal accomplishment was that I managed to get through my schooling while being in this relationship. It felt impossible most of the time, but I did it. My aunt Becky was hosting a small graduation party at her home in Chicago and

John and I planned on leaving in the morning so that we would make the party the night before my graduation. John let me know that we would be driving his dad with us as well, which did not make me happy, but I do not really think it made John that happy either.

When we picked John's father up that morning, he was excited to go to Chicago with us and brought an entire cooler full his homemade apple pie, the kind you drink obviously. I begged him to not open any on the drive there, but he ignored me and started drinking a half hour into the trip. I remember being about twenty-five minutes from my aunt's house when I got pulled over for speeding. I had not been drinking but I was still scared that John's father had open containers in the car. Regardless of his belligerent behavior, I got a ticket and nothing further. Once we arrived in Chicago, we checked into our hotel room that I had bought for us and unloaded all of our belongings before heading to my aunt and uncle's house. John's father was already making racist comments in the lobby of the hotel, which made me want to punch him.

"Can you please get a grip on your father, just for ten minutes?" I snapped quietly at John.

"You know how he is," he whispered back angrily like I was the pile of garbage.

"Dale – stop talking," I snapped under my breath.

John's father stopped talking. I really despised this man, and for many more reasons that the fact he was a racist pile of trash. Not only did he not even try to strongly reenter John's life until recent years, but he treated John's mother like garbage. When the time came later on that I finally left John, his father also continued to contact me and try to get me to come to his house secretly. That all on top of the fact he was a raging alcoholic. Once we arrived at my aunt and uncle's, we got setup in the driveway and the back yard to visit and celebrate my graduation. My uncle had barbequed, and my aunt had gotten some of my favorite drinks. I want to say we had been there for about 45 minutes before John's father had chugged so much apple pie that his eyes were rolling back while he laid very still, mumbling, on my aunts lawn chair.

"Hey, I am going to take him back to the hotel." John said to me.

"Okay! Great, when will you be back?" I asked.

"I am just going to stay at the hotel." John said.

"Wait why? This weekend is about MY graduation," I said, starting to feel like I was going to cry.

"Relax, I will see you later." John said, while he helped his father get to my SUV.

"Guess I will get dropped off later, bye." I said.

I stayed and spent time with my family that had drove many hours to see me. Around 8PM, my mom, stepdad, and sisters gathered their things and we all drove to the hotel. Once we arrived, I walked straight to the bar. My mom asked me if I wanted to come and swim with the girls, but I really just wanted to be alone with a $20 martini. I texted John after about 15 minutes and told him I was at the hotel bar having a drink. After I finished my martini, I reluctantly went up to the room we were sharing with John's dad. When I walked through the door, John stared me down and made it clear that he was angry I went to the hotel bar.

"What is your problem?" He asked.

"You and your drunk father ditched my party. Forgive me for being angry and wanting to have a drink, alone," I said back to him, unpacking my suitcase.

"You are ridiculous. I am going to bed." he said, marching into the bedroom.

"Hey, I'm really sorry." John's father said to me from the living room of the suite.

"Dale it's fine, really. Don't worry about it," I said, grabbing a towel to go shower.

"No, I'm not just sorry for getting drunk, I'm sorry for how my son is towards you. I didn't raise him like that," he said, smiling.

"Yeah, well you really didn't raise him at all." I said while I entered the bathroom.

I ran a bath because the running water would be loud enough that hopefully John and his father would not hear me sobbing. I felt so stupid crying as hard as I was, but I was not even remotely excited for tomorrow anymore. Having John not show that he cared about my hard work just hurt. I stood hunched over the mirror for a long time that night. I let the water run with the drain open and let steam fill the bathroom. My tears and anger were coming in waves. Just when I thought I was done crying; I would get sad all over again and start back up. I kept staring at myself in the mirror trying to remember good times with John, and get excited again for what tomorrow would bring, but I could not seem to find any spark.

The following day I woke up, actually showered, and let my hair air-dry while I put on my makeup. I felt heavy and ugly that morning, but I did my best to hide that. I explained to John that we would all drive to the graduation hall together, and then he would need to go sit with his father until it was over. I did not have any friends at this school and that made standing backstage for 2 hours extremely hard and lonely, especially with how I had already been feeling. A girl approached me about halfway through our waiting period and started small talk with me, and we instantly loved each other.

"So, it's been like 90 minutes and no one has come to stand between us, so I think we are probably sitting together," she said.

"Good! You can get me through this." I joked.

"Honestly, I originally came over here to talk to you because you looked so sad. It was starting to make me sad." She joked.

"That obvious, huh," I said quietly.

"Yeah. If you want to talk about it, go for it. If you want to just keep talking about other stuff, then talk about other stuff. Either way, you are graduating today. That's awesome, right?" She said, clearly trying to get me to show a genuine smile.

"Yeah. Yeah I am. Thank you." I responded, appreciatively.

This girl and I never even exchanged names, we just kept talking until I felt better. Before we knew it we were up to walk across the stage. I stood there, 3 people back in line, watching the hot lights beam in through the curtains. I could not believe I really did it. I graduated college. Finally, happiness started feeling present in me. I was smiling, organically. They called my name, and I walked in stride to shake hands, and smile at the camera. My family was screaming and clapping from the stands, and I felt like I had finally done something exactly right. The best part of this day was that not only did my family come, but my best friend Melanie, her husband, and Liam also came to celebrate me. They did not have to drive those 3 hours, but they did. For me. These three did nothing but show me that they loved me and most of the time, it was a heavy part of what kept me going with a smile on my face.

John approached me as I ran out of the stadium way before the ceremony was over. I really did not care to sit through every single person walking across the stage, as awful as that may sound. When I entered the lobby, John came up to me holding a teddy bear that he had bought from a stand by the front doors and told me that he was proud of me. He also handed me a little bouquet of flowers they were selling. This was literally the 3rd time in almost 4 years that he had given me flowers. I found out the following year that his father made him buy the flowers and teddy bear for me. We all took pictures and said goodbye to each other while we walked to my car. Melanie, her husband, and Liam wanted to go to the Candy Factory, one of my favorite bars, before heading home. I had planned on bringing my sister home with us for 2 weeks to stay with my grandparents, so I had my parents meet us at the bar to hand her off and load her things into my car.

After saying goodbye to my parents, I took my sister into the bar, which was also a restaurant, to meet up with John and the others. John's father was already on his second drink within the 20 minutes we had been there and was already embarrassing me. I downed my drink and let everyone know how much I appreciated them coming, and let John know that I wanted to head home. He looked at me annoyed and quietly whispered to me that I was the one that wanted to go to the bar, so we were going to stay for another drink. My happiness was already evaporated looking at how John's father was acting, and now I was stressed because my sister would have to ride in the back seat with John's father for 3 hours. I went to the bathroom and cried for a few minutes, which sounds stupid, but this was my day. I cannot put into words the glances and stares I got from John for no reason that made me feel how I felt. He was constantly looking at me like he hated me.

Once I wiped my eyes and fixed my makeup, I reentered the bar and finished my drink with a smile on my face. Everyone finally agreed to leave and head back to town, but Melanie wanted to get a quick picture of John and me. John put his arm around my shoulders and smiled. I put on my usual fake smile that hid a million words, and let another false memory be created in film. We drove back to town and dropped John's father at his house, which was a huge weight off of my shoulders. I could take that man in small doses, but that was it. We took my sister to my grandparents afterwards and then headed home. I was quiet that night and luckily John did not bug me about it. The next couple weeks with my sister were peaceful and I had a great time doing things with her. John and I did not fight one time, so it was the best two weeks I had experienced in quite some time and it was over way too soon.

We knew that our lease would be up and available for renewal in July, so we decided that we wanted to start looking for a house together. This was the second most insane thing we could have done next to having a child. There were so many unresolved issues we had that I cannot count them on both of my hands and feet, yet this was what we wanted at the time. John had told his mother what we were planning, and she immediately told us to move in with her after the lease was up so that we could save up some money for a down payment. I told John that as financially smart as this sounded, it would be extremely difficult to have me, John, his little sister, and his mother living under one roof without inevitable tension. John shrugged me off and said this was the plan and I needed to wrap my head around it and act grateful.

I did not need to act grateful; I was grateful. His mother usually dropped whatever she had going on to help any of her kids if they needed it. I did not understand him even telling me that I needed to 'act' grateful because if anyone showed this woman more gratitude than I did, I had not met them. Days were passing like cars in the night anymore, and I felt like I was in a haze most days. We were packing up small things and cleaning as we had time to prepare for our move into his mother's house. When the day finally came, I felt what I can only describe as scared. For what, I don't know exactly. I felt nervous about his mother either seeing the monster he was, or worse; him putting on an act. The evening we finished clearing the apartment out, I told John to head out and that I would fill my own vehicle with the last few boxes.

I stood in the empty apartment in silence, just looking at the marks on the walls. In the living room, I saw the scrape on the wall from when John threw his phone when I told him I wanted to leave him a few months ago. Walking back to the bathroom, I saw the small one-inch horizontal gash behind the door from him whipping it open because I was trying to cry alone in the bathroom after a huge fight we had. Something I wish I would have realized at the time was how horrifying and exciting this relationship with John was. Exciting is not always a good thing as strange as that may sound. Calm and safe is what I always wanted, and more so what I really needed. It's so easy to mix up love and possession, and that burns to think about looking back on those years; that I loved him, and he just could not let me go for the simple fact that he did not want to have to start over and find another woman to put up with him. Even now, remembering everything he did to me mentally, I understand why no one in his life saw that side of him; he had mastered not taking fault or blame for anything.

Heading back to the game room you can see the marks where the TV was before I moved my computer there. The marks were from when he got angry that I was going to my friend's house after a fight and he smacked the TV into the wall. Lastly, I entered the bedroom. The tears I cried in this room could fill a bathtub. I just felt cold standing in here alone. Where are we going? This is my perfect excuse to leave, this is the best window I could have asked for. John is going to be with his mother, and I can leave without him being able to blame me for any financial ties. There would be absolutely nothing that he could use to guilt me into staying with him at this point. I remember walking the perimeter of the apartment praying and asking for guidance, because I knew that after his mother's house would be the biggest financial situation I would ever get myself into, and that was buying a home with John. Yet I got in my vehicle and drove to John's mother's with a smile on my face and sweat on my chest from carrying all of the remaining boxes.

"Last one!" I said, faking excitement as I piled the small box of miscellaneous pots and pans into his mother's garage.

"Let's go to bed." John said with a smile.

I hated this decision so much in this moment. It hurts knowing that no matter what words I write down, the moment cannot be felt by anyone else. The thickness of the air I was breathing after forcing myself to stop crying on the way back mixed with the condescending attitude John had carried all day was more than enough to exhaust me. We both showered separately and climbed into bed in our new apartment, which was the lower level of his mother's. I remember this night well because of how he acted, and how it made me feel. He was facing away from me, which was the usual, and I felt that I needed to say something to fill the air.

"This is going to be good, right? We are going to be good," I said softly.

"Depends on you." he said and fell asleep.

Depends on me. Three words that applied to our entire relationship were finally spoken by him. When he said this to me, little did John know, I got wide-eyed and started to reevaluate many situations that had happened with us. *Depends on you* felt like it weighed 1,000 pounds, and that weight had been on my shoulders since 2013, but just made itself visible by being spoken. I could touch it, and once I could touch it, I could start to figure out how to lift it. I tossed and turned that whole night trying to rationalize his behavior, his words, his actions, and the evidence of him actually loving me. I was up almost all night working on that evidence, long after I wanted to. There really was none. That sounds awful, admitting that there was no actual evidence of him caring about me. How could I stay with someone for years with no tangible evidence of him loving me? The sad thing is, I did not feel that I needed it at the time because there he was. If he did not love me, he would not be here, right? Wrong. So, so wrong. I would think like this to try and breathe life into something that never had a pulse.

I kept going back to the night he messaged me. I did not ask for this torture, I did not ask to be hated, and I did not ask to be possessed by a man that refused to recognize his own damage. That is the thing with narcissists, they do not see their actions as wrong. Their friends and family usually do not see it either. Thus, you finally leaving and then being labeled as the "crazy ex-girlfriend". You hear that term all of the time, more often than not. When you hear it you just laugh it off, but have you ever really thought about who is saying it to you? I heard this line the first month I was with John, and I really thought his last girlfriend, his only other actual girlfriend prior to me, was crazy. She was not. She turned out to be one of my old friends that I had not seen in many, many years. This woman is not crazy, period. In fact, I found out once John and I finally split that he tried to connect with her and she had turned him down to get together. When I found that out, I felt rather good about myself considering John had clearly gotten too scared to try and find someone new to mistreat for a short time. John had told me so many times how she was terrible before I informed him that I used to be best friends with her. After I told him that, he stopped saying anything about her. They had also broken up more than five years before I had even met John, so the fact that he even talked about her told me that it did not end how he said it did.

These types of people will do this; they will tell you that you are perfect and that everyone before you was a train wreck. Do not listen to that garbage, because it is not true most of the time. I will admit, in the few times I have felt it was necessary to bring up John to my fiancé today, it has been to explain why I feel the way I feel about certain actions. I have never called John crazy or obsessed because I know he was not crazy. I was dealing with a self-centered, narcissistic, pathological liar that could not find a way to love me the way he needed to. That's not a sickness, it's ignorance.

When we woke up the next morning, I knew this was just going to be a phase I had to white-knuckle my way through for a while. We had spoken about our projected time here and decided it would be about

5 months. We moved into John's mother's in mid-July hoping to find a home by December. John arranged with his mother that we would pay about $100 a month to help her out and obviously get our own groceries. I was prepared for living here to be hell, but it was amazing for a while. I would cook and clean with John's mom and we just got along great. John's mother's home was a split foyer. Once you walked in the front door, you either walked up the stairs to where her and her youngest daughter lived, or you walked down the stairs to the finished basement where John and I were staying. There was no game room for John, which became severely annoying to me ironically. Once you walked down the steps, you either walked straight into the laundry room, or you turned left, and you are in the living room that we created. Then right behind the living room area was where we put our bed. If you had a birds-eye view it was basically an L-shaped room. It shocked me immensely that being confined to a smaller space actually did not make things worse than they already were between John and me.

The summertime flew by for us and it was probably the most peaceful season of our relationship. John's mother loved to have barbeques, parties, and late-night get-togethers in the back yard. Almost every weekend I was in the back yard helping his mother grill or just hanging outside getting some sunshine. My mood was the best it had ever been because I was not around John as much. He hung out in the basement and would come upstairs if we were cooking or if I begged him to spend time with his family. Before I knew it we were at the end of summer and we still had not found a house that we loved enough to move forward with. I was frantically looking for open houses and walk-throughs online, but I had not found the one yet.

John's mother was single and had been for some time. She divorced John's father many years ago, and for incredibly good reasoning. I had been around him many times because John's parents were particularly good at getting along and keeping the peace to participate in family celebrations. John's father was a drunk mess well over half the time. John loved his mother so much, and I saw that. Obviously, that is a good thing, but occasionally his actions or words towards her were still alarming to me.

Lately, I had been looking at houses online and in the newspaper constantly. I loved living with John's mother and little sister, but we needed to have a place of our own again. It was October now and I had not gone out in quite some time. John obviously was not going out either because the only times he would do that was if his friends asked him to or we were fighting, and neither of those things had happened recently. We have been in this basement for roughly three and a half months, and John had gotten really good at silent yelling. When he would get mad at me, he would still get red in the face and flail his arms, but he would make strong eye contact and just silently and rapidly move his lips so no one upstairs would hear us. All too often I was finding myself either crying in the bathroom, or pretending I was tired and just forcing myself to go to sleep as to avoid any arguments with him. It is hard to write the feelings that I had being this close to him every night.

It is more difficult to put into words how harmful his hateful stares at me were when he would be unhappy with something I said or did. I just felt so worthless at this point in my life that dying crossed my mind a few times a month, and that is no way to live.

Being as it was October, that meant it was our annual Halloween fight time. I am of course being sarcastic as I did everything in my power to approach him nicely for us to do something that night. This time, John actually did not turn me down and I filled with excitement. That excitement dropped just a notch when he told me he would agree to go do something, but he wanted to go to the haunted forest with his buddy and his buddy's girlfriend. I did not want to do that in particular, but I was not going to pass up finally going out together on Halloween weekend. I got ready, which took about an hour, and came out of the bathroom glowing with happiness.

"Are you going to put on a costume or something? I can do your makeup!" I said jokingly.

"No, he said they aren't going anymore so I don't want to go," he said.

"I got ready, you said we could do something together, please?" I asked sadly.

"I mean we can go I guess but I'm not wearing anything," he said, annoyed.

"What if you wear a jersey, and I just put two stripes on your cheeks, so people know you are a football player," I said, trying to get him excited and not annoyed.

"I'm not dressing up! You are not doing my makeup! That's it!" He said, raising his voice.

"Alright, sorry," I said, while walking back into the bathroom.

I was crying softly while removing all of my makeup. Why is he like this? Why is it so hard for him to just do something to make me happy without a blowout for no reason at all? I stood there looking at myself in the mirror, sick of seeing so much sadness in my face, and decided that I was not staying home with him that night. I got into normal clothes, wiped all of my makeup off, and texted my girlfriend Stephanie to see if I could come over to her apartment for the night. Stephanie lived in the apartment building that John and I had just left. Stephanie and I grew close in the time that we lived in that building and became quite good friends. She said she would love to have me and to come over whenever I wanted. I opened up the bathroom door and let John know I was leaving for Stephanie's. He shook his head and looked at me in disbelief. I stared at John waiting for him to attempt defending his attitude towards me and destroying my happiness about spending time together on Halloween weekend for the first time in years. But he said nothing. He stared at me in disgust, and then turned on the TV.

I left and headed over to Stephanie's. When I got there, I was surprised with additional company; a mutual friend of me and Stephanie's. I was so happy I ran up and hugged them both. We all grabbed a drink and sat on the couches to talk about our relationship issues. Stephanie just got out of a really rough relationship with a woman that she was still working with. I remember many nights when Stephanie was sobbing alone in her apartment and she would text me to come over and just rub her back and let her cry. I watched her heart break and knew that I could not fix it, but I sat with her anyway. Stephanie knew how rough my relationship with John was and would check in on me from time to time. Our other girlfriend Laila also lived in those apartments, so that was how we all knew each other. Laila filled us in on her horrible relationship that she was trying to find her way out of as well. I sat quietly and listened to them both.

After a little while, Laila and Stephanie noticed something was wrong and started to poke at me trying to figure out how to make me feel better. I explained to them what had happened, not only that night but for most nights for the past few years. They both stayed fixed on me and looked like they were shocked, because they never saw that behavior from John when they were around him. This is something that just kills you, because you get to describe an absolute monster to the people in your life, and a lot of the time you may as well be describing the boogie man. However, the girls believed me and let me cry. The more I spoke, the harder I sobbed, and the harder I sobbed, the realer it felt. The fog was not as heavy around my head because I was not around John, and I was starting to feel an internal battle between anger and fear. Then something just snapped, and it was like I was back in my car the night John found out about Sam. These were completely different circumstances, but the feelings of fear and anger were identical. I was angry that he would not let me go, and I was scared for the same reason.

Remembering the events that happened next that night still hurt and made me anxious. I remember leaving Stephanie's letting her know that I was perfectly fine and that I was just going to head home and sleep. I really wish I would have done exactly that, but my sadness had taken over me so strongly at that moment, that I could not sit and pretend that I was not drowning inside. I had to get away from John for so many bigger and more severe reasons than just bailing on a Halloween plan. I had to get away from John because I could not find myself anymore. I had almost nothing that I could recognize inside of myself that had not already been clawed by John's words or actions. I had been bleeding for years and I felt like for some reason, this stupid and seemingly meaningless fight was the one that did me in.

I drove to the gas station and grabbed a huge bottle of vodka, and I drove to a motel on the highway uptown. I checked in and found my room while I was texting with my mother and stepfather. My plan was to have one last conversation with them, write a note, drink until I was almost blacked out, and take my own life in the bathtub. I cannot put into words how much my hatred for myself back then makes me sick today. I did not know then what I know now; that it could get better. I would give almost anything to go back to the morning of December 10th, 2013 and tell myself to not answer John's message. In fact, if given the chance to change anything that has ever happened to me in my life, including the sexual assault I suffered years ago, it would still always be that moment that I would take back.

My mother had incredibly good intuition and she could tell just by my lack of emotion in my text messages that something was not right. When she feels that way, she has my stepfather call me because she knows I would never ignore his call. She knows I answer every time. When I answered the phone, I had only taken one sip from the bottle and set it on the dresser. I had superficial cuts on my side from a few moments before I answered the phone. Looking back, I feel like I was punishing myself further and doing it by being in control of physical pain. John already had dibs on my emotional pain, so this was all I felt like I had left. I listened to my stepfather telling me how important I was and that this fight with John was not important enough to cry in a motel over. I actually stopped crying, but before I knew it I had cut my hip and it was too deep to ignore. It was like I was on auto-pilot and my brain hadn't caught up to my body and thought rationally.

I panicked and told my stepfather I had to hang up the phone and call 911. Once I hung up I called and told the operator I needed to go to the hospital. After about 10 minutes, 2 cops entered the hotel room and walked me to an ambulance where I passed out. Not many people knew this story until now because of how ashamed I was; am. This evening and these actions are a violent blur to me now and I, like you perhaps, do not understand why I did it. I do not understand why I had to take my own pain out on myself. I never will understand my hatred for myself and my inability to just leave John alive and in one piece. When I woke up at the hospital, a nurse informed me I had only been passed out for about 10 minutes and that a doctor would be coming in to stitch me up quick. I knew that I would also have to explain my cowardly actions to yet another doctor and convince them that I did not need to be admitted to the ward for suicidal tendencies.

"Miss, your phone is ringing. A John is calling you." The cop said handing me my phone.

"No. please just put it down." I asked.

"Alright," she said and placed the phone on the bedside table.

About thirty minutes went by and I was stitched up and extremely tired. A nurse entered the room and told me that I could sleep there for the night but that I had two visitors here to see me. I panicked and asked what they looked like and the nurse described John and his mother. I told her to please turn them away and say that I could not have visitors. I am sure that she did not actually say that to them, but whatever she said got them to leave. As fast as my heart was racing and as heavy as my heart was, I managed to close my eyes and fall asleep. When I woke up in the morning, I realized that it was a workday today and that I was already late. My phone was dead from not charging all night, so I used the phone on the wall to call John since his was the only number I knew by heart. He told me he would not come and pick me up, that he was going to work, and that I could figure it out for myself.

I did not blame him for being angry, but no matter what he ever did to me I never left him stranded. I hung up the phone while trying not to cry; thinking about what I should do next. I rang for a nurse and asked to be discharged as the Doctor on call last night did not find me at risk, which today is a joke to me. I entered the waiting room and luckily there was a charging dock for cell phones. I plugged my phone in and waited about 2 minutes before trying to turn it on. My first call was to a cab because I knew that I would probably have to wait 10 minutes or longer for them to arrive. My second call was to my supervisor and lead at work who were very relieved to hear from me, and that relief in their voices made me start crying immediately. They went into a conference room to put me on speaker so all three of us could talk. I did not go into great detail, but I told them I ended up in the hospital the night before and that I could not make it in. I knew I was going to lose my monthly bonus and be on attendance probation, but there was nothing I could do about that now.

Once the cab arrived, I had it take me to the motel where I retrieved my car and went home to John's mother's. I did not speak to her right away, I just went downstairs to sleep. My side hurt so badly, and I had no idea how I was going to show John I had hurt myself again. The fact that him and his mother showed up at the hospital means that my mother called them after I hung up with my stepfather, so he definitely knew what I did even though when I called him this morning he did not care how I was doing, or at least he did not ask. When John arrived home, he hopped in the shower and then he asked me what happened. I told him how I had felt and what I had done, it did not take long for him to become furious.

"What is with you and cutting yourself?" He asked angrily.

"Before you, I could recognize when something was poisonous and walk away." I paused. "You know how miserable I am, and you don't care. You never change what you do to me, how you talk to me, or how you look at me. You have torn down my self-worth, which I guess I should also blame on myself." I finished.

I had nothing left to say. What I did was stupid, not because it angered him, but because I hurt myself when I did not deserve that treatment at all. He sat there staring at me, disgusted, and finally managed to put on his poker face.

"You have to stop doing this," he said. "I love you, we will get through this, and I will change whatever I need to. Okay?" He said.

I nodded. There was an absolute earthquake inside of my chest that I was trying to conceal. First of all, I did not want to fix this. This man was making me mentally sick at this point and regardless of what I tried to convince myself of; I was mentally unstable. I did not admit that to anyone including myself. Whenever the thought fluttered towards the surface of my mind, I would force myself to think about something else. It was humiliating to try and admit that I let someone beat me mentally for years and that I could not physically walk away from it. Instead, I sat and let it happen until I hated everything that I was. We went to sleep that night with great tension, especially between his mother, sister, and myself. I did not want to go upstairs and explain to John's mother what I had done, or she would think I was actually insane. So, I laid down and forced myself to sleep. I remember being so thirsty and desperate to not have to go upstairs that I was drinking from our bathroom faucet with my mouth.

The next few weeks flew by as I kept shopping for houses for John and I. Insane, I know, but I came to terms at this point with my weakness and the fact that unless John told me to go, I would not be going anywhere. We had looked at a handful of houses, and by we I mean John, me, and his mother. She definitely hovered severely throughout this whole process and made sure that I did not make any decisions because I would not be adding myself to the mortgage. John did ask me a few times why I did not want to be on the mortgage so I told him that I knew my credit score would make this harder for us. In reality, I knew that if my name went on that mortgage I was certainly never leaving. Then the day came where I found it, I found the house.

I did a walk through on my own with the realtor. I will mention that this realtor was actually also John's mother's realtor, so I knew she was not going to be pushy. The house was 1 level, unfinished basement, three bedrooms, one and a half bath, and had a garage. The front yard was not awful either even though the backyard was useless. This house checked everything on John's list, so I went home to tell him about it after getting all of the necessary paperwork. John looked through the photos and information with his mother at the kitchen table while I made something to eat for the first time today in the kitchen. The unsolicited and nonsensical advice she was giving John overflowed into the kitchen as I laughed and ate my sandwich.

"So? Look good then?" I asked over the kitchen divider.

"It looks decent." John replied.

"Can we all go look at it tomorrow?" John's mother asked.

"That would be great, yeah. I will call the realtor," I said, walking downstairs to get my cell phone.

I did feel a sense of happiness, because if John likes this house then I did something to please him; something huge at that. I set up the appointment with the realtor and stayed downstairs to get ready for bed. When John came downstairs, he climbed into bed and told me that I did a good job house shopping and he looked forward to walking through the house I found tomorrow. I felt calm and fell asleep easily that night. I remember having awful dreams that night from what I imagined was coming; continued fights, bigger shared responsibility, having John secluded to a room all evening every evening again, and I woke up multiple times sweating. I was, and still am, a big believer in intuition and subconscious thoughts, and I know now that the part of me that was trying to swim back to the surface was telling me *do not do this. Not with him.*

The following day, all three of us met at the house I had found to do a walk-through. John's first time walking the property was not what I had expected. He was quiet and looked unamused. He found something to complain about in every single room and my excitement was melting away. The realtor was on my side of course because she wanted to sell a house, and we had been doing walk-throughs for months. It was November and we just really wanted to move before it was painfully cold and snowing. After we all said our goodbyes and left the house, I asked John if he wanted to keep looking or if he wanted to put in an offer. John was quiet and deep in thought for the rest of the night, but of the few words he did give me, I understood that he did not want this house.

Another week, and 4 walk-throughs later, John was so annoyed and fed up with the houses we were seeing, and I had not even picked these ones. John and I were sitting in his car after our latest property viewing and he was just sitting in the driver's seat looking deflated.

"What do you want to do?" I asked him.

"I want to see the house you picked out again," he said.

We went over right away since the realtor was right outside of John's car. This second walk-through was different, and I am not sure why. John had a new appreciation for the house and had significantly less problems with the layout than he had before. But that night in that horribly carpeted kitchen, we made the decision to put in an offer. I was jumping for joy and running around like a child. This was it; we were really buying a house. In that moment it was like I had forgotten the past few years because of how big of an event this was. We went home and got pizza to celebrate with John's mother and we were on cloud nine; together. John was smiling at me, the sun was setting outside the living room windows, and I felt happy knowing that something I never expected to happen was happening before my eyes. Who knows what could happen now. That thought excited me and filled me with a great deal of hope.

It took us the typical five to six weeks to complete paperwork, meetings, and finally close on the house. John's mother attended everything with us, which was a little insulting to me as I understood the loan process and what John *should* have done with his mortgage, but she dismissed me and had him agree to a double mortgage right out of the gate. I shut my mouth and watched him sign the paperwork wishing I could get him to listen to me, but he was not going to trust my knowledge over his mother's.

The meeting ended and we were given the keys to our new home. I remember feeling a little embarrassed because we were not married, or even engaged, but my money went into buying the house too, so I called it ours. We arranged to move into the house about a week later with John's family's help and that was it; we were moved into the home that we bought together, picked out together, and would hopefully heal in together. I walked around the house slowly that night, imagining new ideas and paint colors for the rooms. John went straight to the game room to set it up, and well, game. My grandparents had even brought us a Christmas tree to put up since ours had started to age.

The living room was filled with bright lights and the hope of a peaceful and warm holiday in our new home, which is exactly how the holidays always went for us; peaceful and warm. I could not believe it, but our fourth year together had come to an end in such a big way. We were still rolling the dice with trying to conceive, which hurts every single time I say it, and now we owned a house. What was left to keep him excited? I asked myself that question all of the time wondering why after 4 years he had still not asked me to marry him. The fact that the mortgage was strictly in his name was good and bad for both of us I suppose. It was good because if John ever did make the decision to let me go, then I did not have to be drug through the process of legally removing myself from the mortgage. The bad side to this, for both of us, would be if either of us decided to finally end things unexpectedly, it would leave John with 2 mortgages and me homeless. Neither one of us really expected what our final 9 months together would hold, but we moved forward anyway.

Chapter Five
Drowning

We are now in January of 2018 and have been in this house for one month. From the middle of December until now has been a dream. I do not think John has ever been this laid back and kind to me in our 4 years together, and I remember thinking daily that this house really might change things for us. At this point we were actively trying to get pregnant. I was following ovulation schedules on my phone and spending a lot of money, out-of-pocket, at the OBG/YN office for them to run tests and figure out what the best way to conceive would be for us. I had asked John many times for help here and there with the medical bills, but when I did he would throw me about fifty dollars. All of the appointments I ended up having when everything was said and done totaled to roughly 2 grand. John's fertility test cost him $25 and was painless, obviously. When all the tests were over for me and I had tried several rounds of clomid, I was told that I should have been able to get pregnant by now, and that they were not completely sure why I was not. These things can take years with perfectly healthy people, but I cried for weeks over this and eventually just stopped caring.

My daily routine started with me showering and getting ready for work. I almost never packed myself a lunch the night before because by the time my day was

There is no better way to word this, but John never did things for me. He thought that living together took the place of spending time together, chasing me, loving me, and making sure I was okay. And I was not okay; I had not been okay for a long time. The fights grew less and less as I just stopped confronting him or sharing much of my feelings or thoughts. I plastered a face on every day to match the mood John was in and adjust accordingly to control how my day would go. What else could I do? I felt that I was not strong enough to leave him. I knew that he was not going to end the relationship, and he knew both of these things as well.

As those first few months went on, I was drinking a few times a week at home, trying to numb my sadness. I did take up painting again, even though I hated everything I painted. John and I also did little cosmetic remodels to the house when we had the time. I repainted the guest room a beautiful grey-blue paint that I had bought, and I did a terrible job on those walls. No matter what I did, I could not seem to avoid hitting the ceiling on every single wall in that room. After a while, I came up with the idea to paint a three-inch border around the ceiling to try and make the paint look intentional, and that was also a terrible paint job. I laughed and showed John, knowing that I would just need to paint the ceiling, but he was furious and told me it looked bad. I did not care that he was upset, because he never offered to help until I screwed up the ceiling, and by then it was way too late.

We did also have the oven stop working two months after we bought the house, and this was one of those 1960s wall ovens, so I knew that we were going to have to remodel the kitchen. The range was in the middle of the counter with cabinets underneath it, so we made the decision to cut that section of cabinets out and put a brand-new oven there instead. Melanie's husband took care of cutting out the section of counter that we needed, and even though it was not perfectly straight and looked terrible on carpet, it was doable and appreciated. John always talked about wanting to do other projects around the house, but he never saved money. I had a big white board I bought and wrote out both of our budgets on so that he would stop forgetting his bills. The first four months went along just like a repeating movie until we got into summer, that is when I started to pull further away from John than I ever had.

We had argued about things a lot lately, more than usual, and I realized how much he was lying to me. It was not even about important events, which is what made me so angry. I had gone through John's phone a couple times, which I know is wrong, and had seen a few conversations that made me really sad. I would tell John how I was feeling, trying to get him to say what he had done or said behind my back, and he would yell at me and get angry. If I had proof or he knew that I knew he was in the wrong, he would immediately apologize or start crying. I now know that some people just do not have remorse, but just get sorry that they were caught. I know at this point it sounded like I was walking around everyday passive aggressive and unattached, but that is the exact opposite. When I say I was plastering a face on, I mean I was doing everything I could to make John see me pulling away from him. This was the only thing I had not yet tried, and that was slowly showing detachment to see if he would change. Sometimes John would ask me if I was "okay" or if there was a reason I was "moping", which never made me feel any better. We did have a few conversations about how he seemed uninterested in me unless it was right before bed, and he said that I was ridiculous and that I was just not paying attention to how often we spend time together. I guess twice a month was John's quota.

There would be a few times a year John would start a new show with me, but we almost never finished it because he would rather be gaming. I was going out with a girlfriend, whatever one I could find, at least once a week. This sounds like a lot, and it was a lot, some nights I did not even enjoy it. I just thought that maybe if he does not hear me cleaning and coexisting where he could see me, that he would realize he neglected me so much it did not matter if I were actually there in the house with him. There was only one three-hour class a week for the program I was in at school, so if that class got out early I would even go sit by myself in my car in some random parking lot. I just did not want to be in that house anymore.

In April of 2018, I decided to leave my job and actually use my degree to make a little more money. It was one of the hardest choices I ever had to make, because a lot of my coworkers had become family to me. I got a job at an accounting firm, but not as an accountant. I began working in the payroll department, or branch, of this company on April 16th and I really loved it. It was extremely overwhelming, but exciting. My boss was awesome, and I immediately knew that I would love working under her as well, and that was particularly important to me. John's cousin Blake's mother was head of one of the departments here, so I genuinely believe he put in a good word for me and was a major reason I got hired. Things were going well at this job, and even though I still had school to deal with and my home life, things were going well at work at least.

June came around and I decided since it had been a few years, that I would throw a small surprise birthday party for John at our house. I only invited his family over, but I did get a cake and wanted to hang up a few streamers. John had been sitting on the couch watching a gaming stream for a while, so I walked into the living room and told him that his mom needed help with something and that he should head over to her house and help her out. It took about 5 minutes of convincing, but John reluctantly left. I gave way too many signs of what I was doing apparently, because John figured it out and intentionally stayed at his moms longer. John's mom obviously knew what we were doing so she was also annoyed that he was demanding to stay there for a while. Finally, she got him to come home. He walked into the kitchen and rolled his eyes and smiled.

"Thanks. I knew you'd do this." He whispered while walking over to me to take off his shoes.

"Well you didn't have to stay so long if you knew what I was doing." I joked.

"Well I hate surprises," he said and walked away to greet his family.

He did not hate surprises, he hated not being in control. I am not sure why parties fell into that category for him, but they did. Spending time with his family was fun, but once they left I cleaned up and tried to spend time with John. Luckily, he did not want to go to the bars, but I remember us going to bed early that night after not really doing anything together. I was simply happy that I got to see everyone in his family that I loved and that I had gotten such a cool cake. The rest really did not matter that much to me, because I had learned to not expect gratitude or appreciation for anything I did anymore.

I was sad every single day, even if I did not show it. I was sad that there was no engagement in sight, and that there never would be. I was sad that my body was not letting me get pregnant, because sadly I still thought that a baby would fix this man. Mostly, I was sad because I was starting to tell myself, "You really aren't good enough, are you." And I was believing it, more now than ever. Somehow, John had managed to burrow so deep inside of my head, that he did not leave room for anything else. Church was not even important to me anymore, and that made me hate myself so much. Over the years of us being together, I had asked John so many times to come to church with me, and he said no all times but three. None of these three times he went with me were for a special occasion, but they were because we had fought the night before and he did not know another way to apologize.

The end of summer was a rough time for me because my grandmother that lives in Florida had a health scare. I do not remember exactly what had happened, but it was something in her brain that needed surgery. I kept informing John that I was needing to go see her and asked him if he could take one day off of work to travel with me, but he said no multiples times. If I wanted to take a last-minute trip to Chicago, or if I were taking him to a football game, John would drop everything he was doing to go with me. However, if we were going to be traveling somewhere that did not interest or benefit him, he would ask to stay home. John abandoned me when he got me pregnant and I ignored it. He also abandoned me the night I found out my parents were moving away and let me cry alone. Now, I was worried about my grandmother and needing to see her, and he wanted to stay home.

Once my grandmother had her surgery, I bought my plane ticket and made sure to take the following Friday off of work. John did offer to take me to the airport, which he thought was very chivalrous. I kept hoping between the day I bought my plane ticket and the day I had to leave that maybe he would at least fake a little humanity and come with me, even though he did not want to. That never happened, and the day came for me to leave; alone. I was very silent on the way to the airport, which was about a 25-minute drive from our house. John had the radio on, and I just kept trying to elbow my way through the thoughts that kept flooding my head to remain in a somewhat relaxed state. *Why does he always punish me with loneliness?* I found myself constantly wondering. Other than the night he left those bruises on my arm, he never physically harmed me again. However, the mental torment almost felt worse, because I started to feel like I could not trust my own thoughts or feelings anymore.

"Why are you so quiet? You aren't going to see me for like four days." John said laughing.

Yes, and I can't wait for this time alone. I wanted to say back to him, but that was not what I said.

"I just wish you were going with me," I said, quietly, watching the fields of nothingness pass by my window.

"I told you I don't like not sleeping in my own bed, and you can spend time with your grandma alone that's a good thing, right?" John was great at highlighting what he saw as beneficial circumstances and omitting the negativity of his actions or words. He was a pro at it.

"I guess," I said.

John pulled up to the airport and gave me a hug and kiss goodbye. I did not even want to touch him at that moment, but God forbid I would have shown that, or I would have several hours of a text message argument on my hands. I watched John pull away and I lit a cigarette. The airport here is smaller than an Old Navy, so I knew it would only take five minutes to get through security and wait for the plane to arrive. Leaning up against the side of the building as I watched John leave I just kept thinking about how the further away he was from me, the thinner the fog was in my brain. That's the problem with this type of fog, it starts in your heart, then it moves to your brain before you know it is even there. Then it gets heavier, and thicker, and you find yourself just surrounded forgetting which direction you came from. That makes it so much harder to decide which direction to move toward to get out.

"I wish this was the last time I was looking at your taillights," I said out loud while I put out my cigarette and walked into the airport.

I was sitting in the one and only gate at the airport waiting for the flight. It was just me and a father and his son waiting for the plane. The little boy had to of been about five or six, and he was playing with a little monster truck. He started crying because he could not get it to do something, but I was not sure what he was trying to do. He looked up at his father from his knees and asked him why the toy was broken. I remember this because there was just so much sadness in the boy's voice. His father looked down at him, grabbed the truck, and smiled.

"Buddy, just because something doesn't do what you want it to, doesn't mean it's broken," he said and handed the truck back. "Look at all the things it *can* do," he said, as he got on the floor with his son.

This moment is one that I will never forget, because as silly as it may sound, I saw myself in that little boy for a minute. I saw myself on my knees, asking John what was broken in me, which I had actually done a few times in the past when he had torn me down too hard. This was what I needed; I needed John to tell me *I love who you are, not who you aren't*. I stared at that man and his son for a few moments without realizing it, seeing that he was teaching his son that you do not need to fix something that is not broken. This moment stayed with me and I have thought about it many times since that day. I already knew, sitting in that airport, that being relieved to be without your significant other was not how it is supposed to be. This was the wrong kind of love.

I boarded the plane and had a great time in Florida with my grandmother and her husband. We walked along the beach and had drinks by the shoreline, and I felt free for a few days. When the day came for me to fly home, I felt nothing but heavy knots in my stomach to return. I had tried to not talk to John that much while I was gone in hopes that he would genuinely miss me. When I landed at the airport, I grabbed my bags and went out front to look for John. Of course, he was a few minutes late, but I did not mind, it gave me time to have a cigarette before he got there to hopefully calm my nerves. My body just felt heavy, but I kept telling myself I was jet-lagged. Once John arrived, he helped me get my bag into his car and we headed home. I asked him what he had done while I was gone, to which he answered gamed and slept. Shocker. I did expect to come home to the house being a mess, but when I walked in it was not as bad as I expected. I was not sure which was more irritating to me, the fact that he knows how to clean but never does, or the fact that he really did not even do that good of a job.

We started a new week and stayed on our usual schedules and falsities with our relationship and daily life. I was starting to feel my body image issues bubble up lately, as they usually did around summertime. I wanted to start working out regularly again and was going around the house one night to see what exercise equipment I actually owned so that I could just do what I needed to do at home. I knew that I had an exercise band in a box in the closet of John's game room, so I was rummaging through the closet looking for that. When I found it, it was in two pieces. I grabbed it and just looked at John as if my eyes were asking him why he did this instead of my mouth. He said sorry, but he was grinning, lacking all remorse like it was actually cute to do something like this. Apparently he had gotten mad at his game one night and snapped it in half. He had also punched a hole through a coffee table I bought us back when we lived in the trailer. Clearly, the table was not made of wood, but there was a gorilla fist sized hole in the middle of it now, so it remained in the game room.

John had also punched our large, cushioned chair in the living room a few times when his football team would lose. I know that sounds pretty typical of a man watching sports, but it was ridiculously annoying, considering he completely busted the arm of the chair at this point. I felt deep down that John would never hit me, or even grab me again, but I always had a small piece of me wonder if his anger would ever get red-hot enough that he would if I was the closest thing to him. I walked away from him with those two pieces of my exercise band and stepped out back to our deck to smoke. It took me a few moments to realize I was not only still holding them in my hand, but I was gripping them with intense force. I was so emotional, and I could not figure out what I was actually feeling. Was this rage? Was this contempt? Whatever it was, it was nasty, and I felt like I could scream forever without taking a breath.

When I walked inside the house, something happened. It was like everywhere I looked I was seeing in black and white. Not actually of course, but it felt like a light had been turned off and everything inside of this house was just darkness to me. The clicking sounds of John's mouse were filling the hallway and seemed to make the hair on the back of my neck stand up. My mouth felt dry and my eyebrows were sweaty, but it really was not that hot out, and it certainly was not hot inside the air-conditioned house. In that moment I did not know how to get the colors back. I felt no urge to listen to music, paint, or even take a drive. I just did not feel that I cared about anything in this moment, and that was overwhelmingly terrifying for such an emotional and vibrant person to feel.

We are faced with choices every day and battles we can choose to fight or walk away from. No matter how many times you try to mentally prepare for something, certain circumstances change, and you find yourself caught off-guard anyway, so I found that I did not benefit from preparing myself for anything anymore. This was a harsh moment that felt like it would never pass for me, when all my colors were finally drained. I walked around that house in the middle of the day and was in the dark. The rooms seemed to be so much smaller than they had felt before. The paint on the walls looked thick and unevenly painted. I was no longer in love with this house because it looked like a prison. I knew that day that somewhere inside of me, strength of some kind was bubbling up to the surface. I still had no plan consciously to leave or to even have a talk with John, in fact he seemed smaller to me that day too. He was no longer this life preserver that I felt a need to cling to with white knuckles; he was the water around me. And I was tired of being so close to drowning.

Chapter Six
Jumping

I woke up that morning, the last morning, and it felt normal to a point. We had reached September, and it had been a silent and uneventful month since I had my black and white moment. I remember constantly having this swimmy feeling in the back of my head, like there were two parts of me: one that felt capable of living in hopeful misery, and one that had drastically different plans. There is no way to word this without sounding dramatic, but I really felt like a part of me broke off and was trying to take control for my own good. Nothing especially climactic had happened in quite some time between John and I, but he knew deep down that something had changed in me, and for the first time he was too scared to poke at it.

"Hey, are we still having date night tonight?" I said as I walked into the living room.

"Sure, Netflix?" He said.

"Well, no I thought we would actually leave the house and maybe go for a walk or a drive." *Is he really going to bail on date night for the millionth time?* I thought to myself.

"Alright," he said, seemingly disappointed.

John got up and took a shower while I cooked breakfast. When he came into the kitchen he grabbed breakfast and thanked me for cooking. The air was so heavy it was starting to make me feel lethargic. I had slept very well and awfully long the night before and had not felt this low in a while, and I had no idea why I felt like this. John stayed in his game room from breakfast, to about 3PM when I finally entered the room and asked when we were going to be leaving this evening. He said to hold on because he was in the middle of a fight, so I waited a few minutes before I just left the room. About 10 minutes later he walked with heavy steps into the living room and slammed down on the couch.

"So, what then what do you want to do?" he asked annoyed.

"Is it that hard to just do something with me?" I asked.

"You're just being weird and dramatic. I don't want to go out or anything so don't ask," he stated while looking at his phone.

I did not want to go out drinking at the bars or do anything crazy. This is what I hated, the fact that John acted like if we left the house we had to go out drinking, when I hardly ever asked for that. I just wanted us to do something together and feel like he wanted to be present in the moment. I was definitely not being weird or annoying and I know that for a fact because I was fully prepared to settle for a walk around the block and whatever stupid movie he chose to watch. I was holding back tears because of his tone and the looks he was giving me. Then it happened, another part of me shifted into gear and to this day I barely remember it happening. It was like that last attempt and wrapping your hair tie around your ponytail just one more time, and then it just snaps in your hand. This was that final time.

I stood up and told John I was done. This seemingly little argument was the last straw, and all I needed after almost 5 years was this one tiny push. It makes sense looking back because John thought that after every wrong-doing or argument, there was a reset button. When in reality, all of those occurrences and words never go away; they are forgiven but they do not cease to exist. It all settles and piles into this heaping mountain of garbage that just smells too bad one day. He looked at me annoyed and told me to leave and that he knew I would be back in a few hours anyway. I grabbed my purse and called a friend to come and get me, and within 10 minutes she was there. I sat outside praying that John would just stay inside, which he did. I ran to her car, hopped in quickly and told her to drive away. I managed to hold tears back until we turned the corner, and I could not see the house anymore.

"Bailey, this time feels different, I can't explain why." I sobbed.

"Because maybe this is the last time, the time you really can't take anymore from him and leave for good," she said calmly.

We drove around for a few hours, and after I calmed down a bit we got a hotel room so that I would have time to breathe and talk to my grandpa about moving in for a while. I knew that I would be starting over, with less money and more debt than the day I met John. This thought scared me to death, but anything was better than having to stay in that house one more day. Lying in that hotel room felt cold and unfamiliar. The colors on the TV felt vibrant and harsh, and the bed seemed to hug me in all the wrong ways. Every time I closed my eyes my heart rate would speed up and my mind would only fill with the few good memories John and I had. There were not many, but for some reason my brain would not play the bad memories; the reasons I needed to leave. I knew what I needed to do, but it felt impossible.

I had been away from myself for so long, that when I finally let the wall down inside of my heart to find her again, she was wounded and angry. That part of me is how I left that day, and I never thank her enough. The side of me that was willingly staying in an abusive situation because I was too scared to start over and give up on the fairytale I built was not the part that was going to save me. The part of me that I pushed down and told to keep her mouth shut, that was the part that pulled me out. She was angry, beaten, shushed, and neglected; just like John had done to me.

Bailey was asleep and my eyes felt so heavy, but they just would not stay closed. Honestly, I did not know if it was worse to be awake or asleep with how scattered and impulsive my thoughts were. The days that followed this one were clouded and awful. I had gone to the house to grab a few outfits and immediate items that I needed to spend a few days away from John and still be able to function and go to work. I would get a text or call from John every few hours for those first few days I was away. The messages hurt to read and made my mental battle so much harder. I begged him to leave me alone so that I could sit and really decide if this was what I needed, but he could not be silent for more than a few hours at a time. John was trying to apologize and tell me how he had not had a real meal since I had left him, and that made me so unbelievably angry whether he was trying to be cute or not.

After those few days passed, and I had cried so many times I did not think I had any tears left, I knew this was it and I could not avoid the process anymore. I had been walking around numb for so long and now that I had to face extreme fear and sadness, I felt like if I looked down I would actually see a knife in my chest. I told John that this was truly the end, and I arranged a time and day to come and load up my SUV. I had told him that whatever did not fit in my car, was his to keep or throw away. He agreed over text message, but when the time came for me to gather my things I was not prepared for how it played out. I had a knot in my stomach as I drove to the house for what I thought would be the last time. I had to turn the radio off because every noise was making me more anxious. I parked my car out front and waited a few moments so I could try to calm down before I saw John. When I entered the house, John was already crying quietly and kept staring directly at me.

"Do you want help?" He asked.

"No, I really just need my clothes and stuff from the bathroom. Can you just go to the game room or leave?" I asked him while trying not to cry.

This was my home, too. We spent years and years talking about a family and owning a home together, and now I had been put into the situation of having to kiss that dream goodbye. I took my ring off and I placed in on the ledge in the bathroom, which is when he started really crying. John followed me into the kitchen where I grabbed a few items that had meaning to me. I had these three wicker baskets my grandma had gotten me for organization in the kitchen, and I only took one and let him keep the other two. I walked past him into the guest room where my closet was, and that is when I saw he had taken at least twenty photos of us and laid them out on the bed like a memory game, face up. The house was silent, but it was like he was screaming, "look at what you are throwing away!" by showing me our few good times together, captured by chance like falling stars.

There was the photo of the 4th of July weekend, just moments before he ran off and disappeared for over an hour only to return and ruin the rest of the weekend for me. There is the photo we took in the photo booth at the bar the night he found out about Sam. There are so many smiles and weak flickering moments that were printed to last forever lying on this bed, staring me in the face. My knees started to buckle a little bit, and I felt my face start to get hot. *I cannot do this; I have to stay,* I thought. *What if he changes? What if it will just take a little while longer?* He was quietly squeezing tears out while standing behind me, and I did not know if they were real or not. If they were real, they were not for me; they were mourning the same loss that I was trying to avoid dwelling on, and that was the dream we had built.

I ran around the house grabbing a few more items and got my SUV loaded up with everything that I really cared about. I told John that all of the furniture, dishes, and décor was his to keep. I was not going to leave that house with any items that we both shared. John sat down on the chaise next to the front door while I gathered my purse and keys.

"That's everything," I said.

"Please don't go, I will change we can fix this, just stay." He begged, pulling me in.

I did not feel sad in that moment, I just felt scared that I may fall for whatever he tried to get me to stay. I squeezed my eyes shut for a second, and remembered what he was, and what he has done to me over and over again. It was time he got his praise from someone else. I pushed him away and ran out the front door. I refused to let myself cry until I got back to my grandparents house. When I pulled into my grandpa's driveway, he was already waiting to help me take everything to the apartment above their house. He looked relieve that I had followed through with bringing my belongings back, because I had already tried to leave many times throughout the years. I fell into his arms as I cried and irrationally begged him to take the pain away; the things we say when we feel like dying.

John had his claws so deep that I know I took a part of him away from himself the day that I left, even though I felt in that moment that I was the one who lost something. It took so long for me to see what I had to gain, and that what I had walked away from was nothing but a life of mental deterioration and torture. I did not lose anything but my early twenties, John was the one who lost everything when he lost me. I did everything I ever could to make him happy, and no one will ever love him as hard as I did. I saw that sometimes in life, you would have to decide between letting your fear consume you or standing up and fighting. All I knew was I was not meeting fear halfway anymore, I refused to. I was done letting myself grow distant to a hallow man in an attempt to get him to care about me, because during my distance I learned my true place in his eyes, and more importantly his heart.

That day ended with my grandpa and I unloading my SUV and me taking all of my belongings that I did not leave for John upstairs to my new apartment for the foreseeable future. This upstairs apartment was fully furnished and was typically used as a guest house when family came to visit, primarily my grandma's son. Once you walked up the stairs you immediately entered the kitchen. After you walk through the kitchen, you can turn right and either go into one of the two bedrooms or the bathroom. If you continue straight, you enter the living room. The apartment was a good size, especially since it was just me living in it. I laid in bed that night, staring at the ceiling wishing that I could see how I needed to get to where I wanted to be. I envisioned myself healthy, strong, and happy. I just did not know how to get there. I laid there, deep in thought, when my hand jumped up to my neck as I thought, *oh no, the necklace.* I was still wearing it. I ripped it off and threw it in an envelope amongst my things to be dealt with later.

The following week was very routine. I would wake up, shower, get dressed, and go to work. Working was easier than I expected because it kept me busy and engaged, as opposed to me sitting bored and being consumed by my thoughts. At least it did for a couple days. I was so unbelievably sad, and I knew that I had to deal with it so that I could heal. I felt smaller than a grain of sand sitting in my desk chair at work, holding back tears so hard that I kept forgetting to breathe, but that was still better than feeling worthless to someone that I tried so hard to love. I knew that I hated who I was when I was with him, and I had to focus on that. John was still texting me, trying to get me to come back to him. He was convinced that since I left so much furniture and other home décor that I was sure to change my mind and return. That was not the case, I had just needed to leave so badly that I could not be in that house around him long enough for me to have time to take everything I wanted.

Now, years later, I still think to myself, "I should have taken that with me." when I need or miss certain possessions. I had just built a beautiful entertainment stand that I bought from Best Buy weeks before I left. It took a whole bottle of wine and a lot of swearing, but I put it together myself and it was beautiful. I really left it because he asked me to. He also asked me to help him with a payment on his new couch after I had left, which I agreed to do. What he does not know is that after I had my name removed from all of the utilities, I was charged over $500 dollars in back-fees from a budget plan that we had agreed to. John of course never tried to bring up the designer watch that I had gotten him, or his ring. That ring was my promise to John two years ago that I would never leave him if things got better. I left it under a pillow one night before I left town for a concert with Melanie. I think he hated that I got him a ring, but I made sure to tell him the exact same thing he told me when he found it. All that ring was meant to say to him was that I loved him, and if I had a ring that meant nothing then he could also have one. The day I bought it; I felt I genuinely wanted to give it to him out of spite.

All just possessions; meaningless to me now. John loved his possessions and showing them off, so I figured why not let him keep them so that he can look appealing to the next woman he traps. That was another reason I made sure I gave him back my ring, so that he could not pretend that I wanted any piece of him in my life anymore. That whole week after leaving John felt like I was dead. I was talking to people, and I was completing tasks, but I felt like I was just floating around pretending to be alive. Somedays I questioned if this was truly better than what I escaped. I started to feel regret, which stung, because I knew in my heart that I had to get away. Trying to battle these insidious thoughts on my own was like trying to lift a house. It felt impossible. Just when I would think I was okay, another memory would get triggered and I would have to try and get my head above water again.

I was still waiting for my colors to come back. My phone was constantly being flooded with fake apologies and desperate attempts at getting me to return. Work was busy, but so dull that it was almost impossible to focus. Things at my grandparents were peaceful and loving, but I felt like a broken record crying to them every night, even though they wanted me to. I hit an extreme low that I did not anticipate, because I thought I had already experienced true misery already, but this felt worse. I did not want to experience physical pain like the times before, I just wanted to remove myself from this hell that I was feeling. I felt like John killed me a long time ago and I was just moving from one moment to the next without a purpose. I had been clinging to my faith and begging God to heal me, but I was not accepting the fact that this would take time.

What I had planned to do was dark and selfish. I have nightmares about it often, but they do not include John. I only tell this part of my story because if I left anything out, no matter how embarrassing and shameful, I would be lying. I spent the next twenty-four hours of that Friday after I left John coming up with how I wanted to spend my last day on earth. What I had decided I wanted to do was spend the night with Sam, because I knew that he did not truly care if I was okay or not and would just let me talk. He had found me on online just one day after I had made a new Facebook. He apologized for everything he had said to me last time we spoke, but I did not care about that. What I cared about was spending the night with someone that could act like they loved me while I acted like I was okay, because pretending was all I knew how to do anymore.

That Saturday, I met with Sam at a house he was watching for his friend while he was out of town. We laid around watching TV for hours and ordered pizza. We laid there and pretended. I was pretending so well, that I almost forgot for a moment that I was laying there with another monster. The months where Sam and I had spent time together in the past were short, but he showed me his true colors. Sam's favorite thing to do was ignore me, because he knew what neglect and gaslighting did to me from watching John do it. So, I laid there, staring into Sam's huge blue eyes, and watched his crooked smile come and go as we talked about anything, but how twisted it was that we were together right now. But I did not think of John one time. I also did not think about Sam, even though he was lying right there talking to me. I was thinking about tomorrow.

When we woke up, Sam and I walked downstairs to the kitchen to grab some leftover pizza before I had to leave.

"Thank you, for letting me spend the night here," I said.

"What now?" He asked smiling.

"Nothing, you know that," I said, zipping up my coat.

"I'll see you when I see you, I guess." He said shutting the kitchen door behind me.

I walked out the door and got into my SUV. I ran home to my grandparents to shower and change before leaving them for what I thought would be the last time. I got into warm clothes and quietly made my way back out to my vehicle. I drove around town for an hour in silence, driving past some of my favorite spots. After a while, I found myself driving to places that made me cringe. I drove to the park where John begged me to stay with him the first time I really tried to leave back in 2014. When I realized where I was, I parked my SUV and got out. There were heavy dark clouds in the sky, which felt fitting. I sat on the rock that we once sat on together, that day I tried to delicately tell John that this relationship was too hard for me. I stayed for a moment, but I had to leave. Then I drove past the hospital, where I had been twice now to be stitched up from coming untethered. This memory made me uneasy, but it did not shake me as badly as I expected. I assume because I have visited the hospital for so many other things that those visits fell in the background for me. Lastly, I drove past my parents' old apartment. I missed having them here so much, but I knew them being here would not have changed anything about what had happened.

It was starting to sprinkle, and the raindrops though few, were large and scared me when the first few hit my windshield. I put the car in drive and headed towards a large park on the river, where I made my way through the back entrance knowing it would be the least crowded. I backed my SUV up to the parking space that overlooked the river at its prettiest spot, and I sat in my trunk looking out the propped-up window. I was listening to my favorite playlist, crying and scared. I had planned to send a few text messages to loved ones and pull the trigger, but I kept pushing it back. *Another ten minutes* I kept saying, crying harder each time. It was like I was waiting for a sign, any sign, that there was another way. However, after some time passed, I just could not do it. Some part of me, no matter how deep, wanted to be alive. It was that part of me that I had not met, because I had not yet heard her song. Completely ignoring my better judgment, I drove to John's. That was the only pain I was brave or strong enough to inflict on myself I suppose. When I got there, I was only a little drunk, but I was stumbling. John was so happy that I came back that he was trying to undress me and put his pajamas on me.

"I'm so happy you're home," he said, while he helped me lay down on the couch.

I still do not remember the majority of that night, other than taking a lot of my anxiety medication in the bathroom. I took enough to make myself drowsy, but not enough to harm myself. I told John that I took the whole bottle so that he would take me to the hospital. I remember feeling shame for entering this house again. It felt like a labyrinth that I just kept getting lost in and ending up at the beginning, ending up at home. It is humiliating to share how broken and desperate I had become, but I cannot change the past. When someone admits to thinking about ending their life, or if they are brave enough to share that they have actually tried to, they are immediately judged. I feel confident saying that because I have lost many friends to suicide, and I get angrier each time it happens. But I would be lying if I said I did not understand it. When I woke up in the hospital, John was not there. I was evaluated and monitored to ensure that I was okay physically and mentally, and I was not planning on lying this time about how I felt. I started this journey to find myself again, and I was going to have to finish it. I told the outpatient therapist everything, including the fact that I had been here two times prior for self-harm. After being evaluated, she decided to see me on a regular basis in the future and released me. Leaving the hospital that afternoon, even though I felt shameful, I felt different. The sun was brighter, and the air felt like silk on my face. I could not help but smile, as strange as it feels to say. I felt happy to be alive for the first time in a long time, and that was because no matter how close I got to the edge, the real edge, I did not step off.

The following night was the last time John and I ever spoke. I knew that I had become someone else in those years with him. I was twisted, pulled, and beaten down inside for so long, that all I could think about for so long was dying. When that seed was planted in my mind, it grew like any organism does. Spreading and feeding on any hope that it could find, leading me blindly into any possible way out. I finally got what I needed, and that was John telling me that if I wanted to die that badly, he knew I had to leave him. John told me that he would really let me go so that I could find happiness again. I made sure to remove all possible ways of communication starting with online, and even though I still know his phone number by heart, I have never and will never reach out to him. A whole year after no contact or reason, his mother even showed up to my grandparent's house, where I no longer lived, to return a single spare key from my old SUV. I was shocked, because there was absolutely no reason that she should have brought that back, but not any of the other belongings that I left behind. Regardless of her reasoning, it did not affect me.

Once I forced myself to smile and remain focused at work, it started to feel like real life again. Before I knew it, I was smiling for actual reasons and I found myself laughing at my grandpa's jokes again. That residual fog after leaving John was the thickest, which was unexpected, but it was finally breaking down. I was starting to do my hair and makeup again, instead of pulling my hair back into a tight bun every morning. I would catch myself smiling at my reflection as I washed my hands in the bathroom at work, simply happy to see colors again. But just because I was able to move on does not mean it was easy. I know John assumed that I was trying to find someone else, but he was still too dense to realize the only person I was looking for was myself. I had no interest in even a casual relationship with another man, and I told myself it would probably be a year before I even thought about putting myself back out there.

I stopped taking my anxiety and depression medication to see what would happen, and I only did this after speaking with my therapist. I had been seeing her for a few weeks and it was going really well. I was always very honest and would tell her about all of the times throughout my week that I would have a flashback or hear a song that reminded me of John, and I would start sobbing uncontrollably. She kept reminding me that this would take much longer than a few weeks, or maybe even a few months to move on from. I kept forcing myself to look the other way when my heart was trying to make me feel. After a little while, I realized that I had to mourn my loss. That felt ridiculous to say out loud when I was talking with her, but I did finally understand what she meant. Just because I left John, did not mean I did not also lose something. I lost a dream. I lost almost five years of my life where I chose misery over happiness. I lost so much. However, I also knew that I would eventually rebuild my life. After about two weeks of no medication, I felt fine; vibrant even. Actually, today marks just shy of two years since I have been on any medication. I was not the problem, and I finally believed it. I did not hate myself anymore. I saw beauty, and intelligence, and a misunderstood persistence for my happiness. Those traits pose as threats to insecure and broken people, and maybe that was ironically one of the reasons I attracted that type of man.

The most important thing I ever did was forgive myself. It was hard, and sometimes it felt impossible, but I forgave myself for everything. I forced myself to face the fact that in a time of desperation, I flirted with being unfaithful. As hard as it was, I would make myself focus on the pain whenever I would get confused and miss John. I would give myself no more than five minutes to sift through my thoughts and move on with my day. I had to constantly remind myself that I did not miss John, I missed the life I thought I was going to have. To make things harder, I have my scars to remind me daily what I had done to my own body, but those marks also remind me that I am still here to see them. That short film in my mind of happy times would start playing without any warning, and it would happen at times that I would least expect it. However, as time went on it stopped hurting so badly. It ends up as a faint cringe. I found it important to stop that short story of happiness, and replace it with the painful ones, to remind myself of why I left. Five minutes to reboot.

As a young girl I always dreamed of finding a man that would love me enough to stay, marry me, build a family with me, and show me every day that he wanted me in his life. So, to try and build that dream with a monster in sheep skin made me want to build a wall so high, and so strong, that I would never be hurt like that again. What I have learned about these walls, is that they do keep the wolves at bay, but they also keep the right people out. It is a hard balance, but I did not let myself build my wall so high that the next man that came into my life would have to pay for John's mistakes. I knew what signs to look for to prevent my heart being broken again.

Chapter Seven
Still Breathing

One day, you wake up and things are simply different. You can plan to leave a million times in your head, but I don't think any of us are ever completely prepared for the day it actually happens. Up until this day, I had planned on just looking at my living options in the near future and telling John that he had worn me down so thin that I felt like I wasn't a person anymore. I did everything I did throughout my day, my months, and my years specifically for him, and when he did not do anything for me, like looking at me or actually hearing me; I got smaller. I did not know what a normal relationship was before I met John, so when he started draining me, more and more as years went on, I had no idea what was happening.

It took me years to finally realize that I had given myself to a man that had already thrown me away. I felt that I could not leave him because the addiction to John was stronger than any drug I've ever come into contact with. It was a mystery for a long time why it took me so long to give up hope on someone that made it clear every single day that I was disposable and used. Why did this man make me feel that I needed him so badly? I still do not have all the answers, and I am okay with that. Finding peace is not impossible, no matter how annoying it is when loved ones tell you, "give it time." Or "it gets easier." They are right. I wanted to scream at every person that told me that for quite some time. I actually gave up on closure almost immediately, because I imagined the hundreds of statements I thought would make me feel better realizing, they would be worse to actually hear.

Being lied to, used, cheated on, and warped for years can and will leave you feeling confused and angry. I hate saying this but leaving was easier than the time I had to spend with my thoughts afterwards, picking up the pieces. Moving throughout my day was like playing mental jack-in-the-box; having no idea when those triggers would pop and paralyze me. Battling the dark and heavy questions and memories that creep from the back of your mind when you do not even provoke them.

I really thought that leaving John meant I was truly nothing now. He took who I was at the beginning and warped me, stretched me, and turned me inside out. I did not know who I was when I left, so how was I supposed to get that woman back? That is one of my biggest points here: do not go searching for who you were, because they are long gone. You are not broken or damaged goods, but you are now someone who may have thicker skin, higher walls, and deeper cuts. You will never be who you were, but you can be better than you could imagine. Your fairytale is not gone, you just got the ending wrong.

I started this book thinking that I had thick enough skin now that my memories would not hurt to relive, but they did and that is okay. Just know that my closure came from a very unexpected place at a very unexpected time, and it felt like I had finally shed layers upon layers of dead skin. It is not hard to want to die when you are submerged in misery, however it is hard to bury that

118

desire to give up and make yourself take the next step forward. I felt as though I had died, many times over while I was with John, and in a sense I did. I kept trying to kill the part of me that was too weak to fight back. Until one day, I did kill her. The person writing this book is not the person John hurt for years. The person writing this book thanks God every day that she went through what she did and came out alive. I would not be here today if I had not held on for just a little while longer.

When times got harder than I felt I was capable of managing, I would whisper to myself, "You're still breathing." And I was. I was feeling awful but I only knew that because I was still breathing. I started to feel my chest get lighter each time I thought this, feeling like I had control even if it was for a few moments. Then one day, without knowing it, was the last time I ever had to tell myself that I was alive, because I did not question it anymore. The same thing will happen with any self-love you give yourself, and you will start to feel new growth from who you used to be. You will grow into a new version of you that is easy to face in the mirror; stronger. Your colors come back, and they come back brighter.

Regardless of the fact that I was not planning to find someone for quite some time, I did. When I was not even looking, he found me. I was not planning to fall in love, real love, but I did. The past two years with him have been everything I had ever dreamed of and more, and because of my past and all of the sadness I went through, I ended up in his path. For that, I cherish my past; no matter how painful it was. Just because you are expected to learn to live with a painful past does not mean you are not allowed to recognize how it affected you. I finally realized that I could not wait out the storm anymore, and

I had to walk through it; feel it. That is when I found myself again. That is when I healed. I wake up happy and calm every morning, not worried or sick to my stomach about fights or being ignored. I know how easy it is to just marinate in the painful memories and the betrayal, but it is never impossible to find your happiness again.

Never stop until you find the right kind of love.

Made in the USA
Monee, IL
11 January 2021